SHADOWS IN THE VALLEY

SHADOWS IN THE VALLEY

THE STORY OF ONE MAN'S STRUGGLE FOR JUSTICE

FRANK A. KOSTYU

DOUBLEDAY & COMPANY, INC.
GARDEN CITY, NEW YORK

DEDICATED TO

Tina and Ed Krueger
and their friends
the
Mexican-Americans

She doesn't feel like an animal, Jesus, even though she's being treated like one

She looks sixty but she isn't yet forty years old. She is a migrant farm worker. She's working in this field all day —and day here means sunrise to sunset. Afterward, she'll go back with her family to spend the night in a one-room tin shack most people wouldn't let their dog live in.

Nothing seems to be gained by her suffering and deprivation, Jesus. She never gets ahead financially. The small amount of money taken in is already owed for back groceries. She needs a lot of medical care she'll never receive. Her husband is just as much a beast of burden as she. Their children seem already to be caught in the same vicious circle of exploitation.

There is still a vision of humanness inside her mind and soul, Jesus, although her body is broken and her face is wasted. Should she nourish any glimmer of hope, Lord, or would it be better for her to erase hope from her consciousness? What happens to a society which takes such a toll in human life and doesn't care?

PREFACE

UNDER a hot, blistering Texas sun a Mexican-American woman has draped a burlap bag over her shoulder. She is picking honeydew melons at ninety cents an hour. The bag holds thirty-five melons of about a pound each. With the addition of each melon, her bag gets heavier. It cuts into her shoulder, and then she straddles the melon rows toward a waiting truck. Up she goes on a narrow plank and gently rolls out her pickings. She pauses, gets a drink of tepid water from a common cup, squats at the side of the truck and heads back to the melon fields.

A young man by the name of Ed Krueger has watched her toil in the hot fields. He has watched a group of people we have taken for granted in this country. They are the Mexican-American migrant workers. Without them, many of the basic foods that we find on our tables would not be there—potatoes, cantaloupes, carrots, peas, sweet corn, onions, tomatoes, cabbage, lettuce, spinach, beans, beets, broccoli and many other vegetables. Neither would we have the profusion of citrus fruits, cherries, apples, strawberries, pears, grapes, and plums. Sugar cane and sugar beets would be hard to come by. These fruits and vegetables find their ways to our heavily laden tables, but we offer scarcely a passing thought to the backbreaking human labor that has gone into bringing them to us.

Ed's heart went out to these people, the brown people, who are disenfranchised Americans. This book is the story of Ed's struggle to improve the lot of the impoverished Mexican-American. For his efforts to do so he was fired because of the antipathy on the part of the established community to his work. It was a refusal of the power structure in the Rio Grande Valley to come to grips with some big problems.

Ed feels that there are many people who believe in democracy in principle, but when it comes down to allowing people to participate in this democracy effectively and meaningfully, these same people don't believe in democracy after all.

It will be up to the reader to decide whether he can point the accusing finger or cast the first stone.

I want to thank Ed and his wife Tina for the co-operation they gave me in preparing this book. My grateful appreciation, too, goes to Cesar Chavez and the staff of the California Migrant Ministry. For all those who added their words and comments in their own ways, I am most grateful.

Above all, I wish to credit my wife Margie for her help. Without her encouragement and nimble typing fingers, the writing of the book would have been difficult. Joel, Paul and Kathy have also helped in their suggestions and especially in their patience when "the book" took precedence over other things.

Frank A. Kostyu

Montclair, New Jersey

CONTENTS

PROLOGUE

A STRANGER was driving with a rancher over a blistering and almost barren stretch of the Rio Grande Valley when an exotic bird scurried in front of them. Asked what it was, the rancher replied, "That is a bird of paradise." The stranger rode in silence for a moment, then mused, "Long way from home, isn't it?"

On my first visit to the Rio Grande Valley in Texas, I realized that this part of our nation is not a garden of Eden. Parts of it are still unwatered and unproductive. Brush and sand blow across the road. In many places as far as the eye can see, there is nothing but the parched brown earth, a weird beauty.

But with the construction of dams, such as the Falcon Dam, and irrigation canals, more and more of the scrubland is taking on a lush, green look. Citrus groves are being planted, and crops of melons, onions, corn and other vegetables are turning former wastelands into agriculturally productive areas. The Lower Rio Grande Valley Chamber of Commerce has described the area in glowing terms: ". . . the four southern-most counties in the state —Cameron, Hidalgo, Starr and Willacy—is a land of year 'round beauty and pleasure . . . On the scenic, well-paved back roads the visitors will see the valley at its best . . . emerald-green citrus orchards and vegetable fields, pleasant small towns in tranquil, semi-tropical settings."

To the visitor looking for things to see and places to go in the tropical tip of Texas, there are pleasant inducements. He will find swimming, golf and other forms of recreation. When the fish are biting at Delta and Bucy lakes, the happy fisherman goes home with his black bass, crappie, channel cat, bream, perch and bluegill. In Bayview are the homes of wealthy industrialists. In San Juan, the famous two-million-dollar shrine on a ten-acre site attracts thousands of pilgrims each year. The shrine has a pilgrim house and cafeterias that serve savory Mexican and American foods inexpensively.

What could be more idyllic than to spend a vacation in such a tropical paradise? This is America's fun-tier!

But all is not so idyllic in the Rio Grande Valley. There are clouds and shadows that bring darkness to the pleasant small towns and hang ominously over the green fields and ranches. I had heard of the problems in the valley which were brought about by new developments, so I went down on numerous occasions to see what was really going on.

When I left the main highways, I saw the tourist areas and the attractive homes in the quaint valley towns, many of which have a population of less than five thousand.

But going off the beaten path, I saw more than quaint towns. I found people stooping and working, burned by the blistering sun. Across the town from those attractive homes there were the dusty, unpaved streets turned into seas of mud during the rainy season, substandard clapboard and adobe houses. There were weary and angry people. There was tension.

In this abundant, fertile valley there lived the Mexican-American farm worker. I drove down a narrow dirt road one morning and stopped at a small dwelling set back in a clump of trees. The yard was swept bare of leaves and bark, but I found the family living in a shack with a dirt floor, without water, without electricity. In the back yard a foul-smelling drainage ditch rippled sluggishly, carrying sewage and human excrement on its way to the neighbors, who would add their share. A well, capped by an old-fashioned pump, was sunk close to the "river" for the family water supply.

The impoverished Mexican-American has qualities that we could all use—friendliness, warmth, concern, the ability to endure. He is a good worker who gives an honest day's work for a paltry sum. Yet we as a nation have been unwilling to upgrade the quality of life as found in the Rio Grande Valley in Texas and the San Joaquin Valley in California, in the Southwest, Florida and other parts of our country. While we as a nation have declared a war on poverty, our major efforts have been aimed at urban poverty, and few programs have had significant impact on destitution in rural areas such as are found in the Rio Grande Valley, an Appalachia-type region where the per capita income is lower than the Appalachian states. We have not been willing to break the shackles of the social forces which confine children to live and die in squalor, that make mothers endure a life of endless drudgery and that treats fathers, at the best, like second-class citizens, and at the worst, like slaves to be manipulated and exploited.

There is something ugly about this, an ugliness made especially vivid because it all happens in the wealthiest nation on earth. There is a deep social malady evident in this part of the world which produces people whose only course is to become migrants.

We eat well and suffer from overweight and are reaping the rewards of booming affluence. But the seasonal farm worker still earns from fifteen hundred to two thousand dollars a year. While we talk of remedying visible evils, he is asking that the nation consider for him better jobs, higher wages, a home of his own and better paying opportunities for his children. It is important to continue to minister to distressing symptoms, but it is essential at the same time to direct an attack on the causes of these symptoms.

This book is a challenge to Americans to become aware of the fact that we live well at the expense of the field worker and his family. He provides the cheap labor for our farms, our stores and our homes. The sacrifice of the worker's dignity keeps some prices low. His low status feeds our sense of well-being.

There is a deep cancer in our national life that compares in intensity, if not in scope, with racial injustice. The life of the migrant farm worker is not known to us.

The focus of this book is on the Rio Grande Valley and the man who has been looked upon by the Mexican-Americans as a friend leading them out of bondage. Ed Krueger has been inspired by events in California, the vineyard workers, the grape boycott and the nonviolence of the charismatic leader of the movement, Cesar Chavez, himself a product of Mexican-American heritage and the soil.

The service of those who would help the farm workers has not been easy. We can see this in Ed Krueger's meeting head on with the Texas Rangers and the Establishment, in his struggle to remain steadfast even when pressured by the leadership of the old Texas Council of Churches. As Cesar Chavez is determined to carry on the fight for a better life among farm workers in California, so Ed Krueger is resolved to remain in the Rio Grande Valley.

CHAPTER 1

Making them what they are

THERE are one million of them! They are a vast pool of migratory farm workers who are a part of the American agricultural scene. They are comprised mostly of Mexican-Americans, blacks and some whites. Every year farm workers and their families leave their home counties to fill the continuing and fluctuating seasonal demand for labor that is so vitally important in our society.

As farm workers from Texas traveled north, one young man who came into contact with them was Ed Krueger. Born in Indiana, of parents who served in the ministry of the United Church of Christ, Ed met many of the brown Americans as a boy. When his father moved to Oklahoma, Ed became interested in the Mexican-Americans who were on their way to the sugar-beet fields in Colorado. He read John Steinbeck's *Grapes of Wrath* and became concerned about these migrants.

Ed's first real confrontation with brown people came after he graduated from Elmhurst College in Elmhurst, Illinois, and Eden Theological Seminary in Webster Groves, Missouri. He went to Honduras to serve in the mission fields there. However, before he left the States, he

MIGRATORY AGRICULTURAL WORKERS

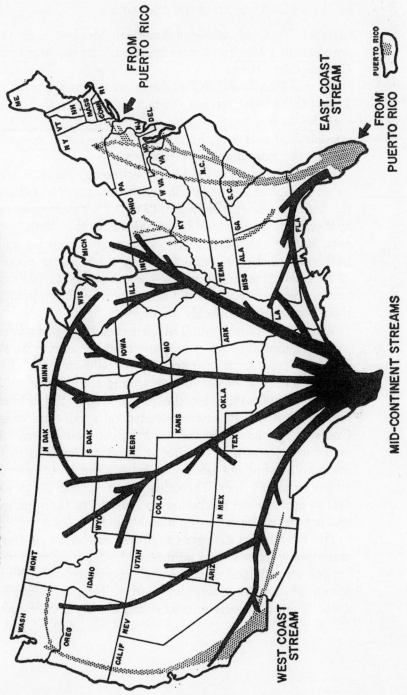

TRAVEL PATTERNS OF SEASONAL

FROM PUERTO RICO

EAST COAST STREAM

FROM PUERTO RICO

PUERTO RICO

MID-CONTINENT STREAMS

WEST COAST STREAM

married Tina, of Mexican-American descent and the daughter of a Mexican-American Methodist minister from Crystal City, Texas.

Ed and Tina found in Honduras what was apparent in Texas—there was a strong distinction between the haves and the have-nots. So when his term of service in the mission field was over, he returned to the States to work among the migratory farm workers.

His search for a job led him to Edinburg, Texas, where he was employed as a public school teacher. His sympathy with the students led him into the villages—or *colonias,* as they are called—where he would talk to the youth, parents, leaders and other farm workers. In school he realized some of the problems faced by these young people of Mexican-American descent—their inability to communicate, their poverty and the necessity of children joining their parents in the fields at an early age.

When the Texas Council of Churches in 1953 assumed some responsibility for a migrant ministry among Mexican-American farm workers, especially in the Rio Grande Valley, it began to look around for a person with suitable qualifications for the job. By 1967 the council realized that two men were needed on a full-time basis. One was to minister to the workers, counseling them on nonviolence, assisting families in need, working in their communities but not becoming involved in labor unions, strikes or picket lines. The other person was to be an expert in agricultural marketing and an aid to farm groups seeking to establish better marketing facilities.

The work of Ed Krueger caught the council's eye. Here was a young man with a ministerial background who was himself an ordained minister, well acquainted with Mexican-American ways, customs and culture, a man who spoke Spanish fluently and who had a wife, herself coming from a Mexican-American background, who understood his concern. Ed was hired to minister to the migrants.

Mr. Krueger has been described as a "handsome, mild-mannered, self-effacing blond with a disarming smile and an almost mystical sense of solidarity with the weak." When I first met Ed, I realized the description was a good one.

With their four adopted Mexican-American children, the Kruegers began their work among the migrant farm workers in the Rio Grande Valley.

There are approximately ten million Spanish-surnamed citizens in our country, over half of whom reside in the Southwest. In 1960 Mexican-Americans represented over 12 per cent of the total population in the five southwestern states; this group is the largest minority in each of these states.

The Mexican-American may be the descendant of the Spanish explorers Cortez, Cabeza de Vaca or Coronado. Or he may have recently migrated from Mexico and may very well be the descendant of the great Aztec civilization. Or he may be a mestizo from the union of Indian and Spanish.

There are others in the United States who have the same features, background, language and surnames. For example, there are the Puerto Ricans, Spanish-Americans (from Spain), Central Americans (from Costa Rica, Panama and elsewhere) and South Americans. Therefore, among the Spanish-speaking Americans we find a diversity in origin yet a great commonality in traditions and language. They have also shared the same problems and experiences as citizens of the United States.

As we have seen on the late-show Westerns, as the Anglo-American moved out into the frontier lands, the

Mexican-American gave way as did the Indian. He lost land which had been a part of his family heritage for centuries; he lost his footing in the community. Instead of governing the village, he became governed. His language became the mark of a "foreigner." Suddenly he found this was neither his land nor his home. He became the victim of pillage, gold, slave-taking and rape. Now he was dominated.

As the years passed, the Mexican-American was pushed into menial jobs; his children rarely reaped the benefits of education. There appeared in towns, villages and cities the poor sections or *barrios*, the ghettos of Mexican-Americans.

How do the highly crowded living conditions affect migrants psychologically? Suppose that four young migrant children spend most of their time in one room with their father and mother. Among other things, they are subjected to a lack of privacy among themselves and their parents. They see their parents, who can not restrict their love-making to private or secluded places, engage in open sexual relations. Living and sleeping so close to each other brings migrant children up in a world quite different from that of middle-class homes.

Dr. Robert Coles, a psychiatrist who did some research for the Southern Regional Council, made some startling observations after living with ten migrant families. Migrant children mature and become adults very quickly. By the time they reach the age of ten, they will have already worked in the fields. I myself saw young boys and girls working in the melon fields of the Rio Grande Valley. They are a part of the family "team." Mother and father work with the older children, while the babies sit on the ground playing or nursing on a bottle.

So those who reach the ages of ten and twelve start be-

coming adults psychologically. They can be seen on buses
and trucks as they move from harvest to harvest with or
without their parents.

We know that school children traditionally have enjoyed an extra measure of security and trust. They can
count on school; it is as regular as milk money and the
daily bus ride to those who live a distance away. This
environment which most of our children are accustomed to
leads to receptiveness and eagerness to learn. We antic-
ipate college and graduate school in their futures. This is
especially so today when so many teen-agers have the
prospect of financial assistance to go on to school. We
declaim that one must have a college education even to
get in line for a job. Migrant children do not enjoy this
security. Usually they are without roots and lead a kind
of nomadic life with their parents as they follow in the migrant stream from harvest to harvest. Thus for the
two hundred thousand educationally deprived children
there is no "little red schoolhouse," no sense of the familiar and the accepted.

Former Secretary of Health, Education and Welfare
Anthony Celebrezze said of the migrant educational problem, "Migrant agricultural workers are often described as
America's forgotten people and their children as the most
educationally deprived group of children in our nation.
They enter school late, their attendance is poor, their
progress is slow, they drop out early; consequently illiteracy is high. Studies indicate that most migrant children
are far below grade level and that their school achievement is usually under fourth grade."

Richard Cardinal Cushing, archbishop of Boston, said,
"We often tell ourselves that in our great country today
any youngster who really wants a college education can
get it if he tries hard enough, but we know this is not

true. Not only in poverty areas, but in many hard-working and self-supporting families of modest means, today's high cost of higher education makes it impossible for children to go to college. We need an efficient and resourceful nationwide organization devoted to the single purpose of helping any deserving youngster, regardless of race, creed or color, to get a college education."

A teacher in a migrant adult-education program pointed out a problem that she faced in her work. "My students know nothing of the real value of education. And even if they could know, they would never believe that it was for them." I asked a young man of twenty-two, born in the valley, why he had dropped out of school. He said that Mexican-Americans just cannot afford to go to school. As soon as they are old enough to stand and stoop over they need to go to work, for the whole family has to work as a team to pool the income resources so that they can live for a year. He said, "Our parents don't want us to go to school, and the schools don't want us either. When I was in my teens some other boys and I talked about going back to school, but we remembered that we never had a teacher who had tried to teach us, so we just forgot about the whole thing."

It is no wonder that at an early age the children of migrants start becoming adults. It is not long before they are marrying and having children of their own. Brides of fourteen and fifteen are not uncommon, and the husbands are not much older.

Before marriage, girls of twelve and fourteen go out at night without their parents' knowing where they are. They may even stay out all night. They may leave "home" quickly, probably as the result of the sexual maturation that comes from crowded living.

Let us consider a typical couple whom we will call

Luis and Flora. As young married adults the couple takes to the fields on the bus at six in the morning. In a short time, they have a child, and the mother accepts the responsibility for the baby and adulthood. In this abundant and fertile valley, Luis and Flora start out their lives together in a shack with dirt floors, without gas, water or electricity. When Luis works for a small grower, he bends at "stoop labor" all day long under the boiling sun, battling insects and pesticides for not much more than forty cents an hour. On days that he works for a large grower, he may for a brief period raise his income to as much as $1.25 an hour. He is not protected by fringe benefits such as medical services, unemployment insurance, job security or workman's compensation. Fields lack toilets. There is no cool drinking water or personal drinking cups. In getting to the job, both Luis and Flora must usually rely on hazardous transportation.

As time passes, Luis wants to take his growing family and try to break out of the migrant-cycle stream. He realizes that he is getting cheated; he is often promised work and the crew chief does not show up. If the chief does show, he may not get to start work until midmorning. He is exploited, and he works hard for a starvation wage. Luis occasionally gets to see television as he stops by the bar. He sees the colorful ads in the magazines, so he knows that there is a better life "out there."

Luis lives in Starr County, Texas, which ranks as the fourteenth poorest county in the nation. A 1966 sampling of interviews with seventy-five farm workers revealed that:

Forty-six workers hoeing vegetables and cotton received forty-five to eighty-five cents per hour, with fewer than twenty-six earning as much as fifty cents.

Thirteen workers harvesting cantaloupes received from fifty cents to a dollar an hour.

Sixteen workers driving tractors received less than eighty cents an hour.

Should Luis go over to a neighboring area? What would happen to him there? According to the U. S. Census Bureau, the median family income for the Spanish-surname family in neighboring Hidalgo County was $2027 in 1960, while the median for the total U.S. population was $5660. Many farm workers earn less than $1500 annually, depending on the span of the work year, the weather and the crops.

The young migrant stands at the bottom rung of the economic ladder. Where should he go to work at that which he knows best—farming? To what place shall he "escape"? While hourly wages to the average farm laborer have increased from $1.14 an hour in 1965 to $1.33, there are ten states (Alabama, Arkansas, Georgia, Louisiana, Mississippi, New Mexico, North Carolina, South Carolina, Tennessee and West Virginia) with an average of about a dollar an hour. Wages range from a low average of eighty-nine cents in South Carolina to a high of $1.62 in California and Connecticut.

So Luis and Flora see themselves able to attain only the lowest annual income of any of America's occupational groups. In construction, mining, lumber and wood products, canning, clothing fabrication, laundries and dry cleaning the average wage runs from over four dollars an hour down to $1.73. Luis and Flora will be fortunate if they get the national average of $1.33. More than likely, they will discover that they are the most poorly paid for what they contribute to health and welfare. So to get some money to enjoy the "good life," they decide to go to

California, unknowingly headed for further disappointment.

When Luis gets to the city, he finds that a lack of education stifles his bid for a job. He faces not-so-sympathetic authorities. For weeks his outlook is merely sitting around waiting for a job. What Luis learns is that he lacks the ability to function as a citizen. He is not aware of his rights, so he does not act aggressively or resolutely.

With funds running low, Luis and his wife move in with a couple of their friends and discover it is no go. He becomes tired of waiting, and one day he moves on because he just does not feel right doing nothing. The passive idleness is not what he wants; it is too much in contrast to the energetic, kinetic, changeable and active life to which he is accustomed.

A psychological change is coming over Luis. At twenty he is a full-fledged adult, yet an older migrant. He is a handsome chap but will age rapidly. Interest in another kind of life eventually begins to wane. He will move about now with his own family and not with his parents. Very possibly he will not see them often again. Like other migrants, he has settled into a combination of industry and initiative that will carry him along the migrant stream looking for backbreaking work, but at the same time a feeling of lethargy and despair of not being able to provide a better life for his family and himself creeps over him. How will his attitudes affect his children?

In his case analysis, Dr. Robert Coles studied the development of migrant children. He found a sharp infant mortality rate. There is an acute incidence of tooth decay, ear infections that result in faulty hearing, heart disease, parasitic diseases that produce a loss of appetite, weakness and anemia; vitamin deficiencies are caused by faulty eating habits; there are diarrhea and fungus diseases of the skin, chronic tuberculosis, venereal diseases, kidney and bladder infections and muscle pains and back injuries brought on by working conditions.

These are merely the physical diseases; what about the minds of these children? When migrant children suffer from not one but a number of these diseases, it is easy to imagine what happens to their mental processes. In early years a child is cheerful, spontaneous, relaxed and affectionate in spite of his hard life and poor health. But as he grows older he harbors hostility and resentment that can be manifested in an ugly mood. He does things he does not understand.

On September 2, 1969, in the Superior Court of the State of California in the county of Santa Clara at San Jose, the Honorable Gerald S. Chargin, the judge, was hearing the case of a Mexican-American minor brought before him on a charge of incest. The defender of the minor was Fred Lucero, the court probation officer was William Topagna and the court reporter was Susan K. Strahm, from whose record the following testimony was taken.

The Court: . . . I just get so disgusted that I just figure what is the use? You are just an animal. You are lower than an animal. Even animals don't do that. You are pretty low . . .

You are no particular good to anybody. We ought to send you out of the country—send you back to Mexico. You belong in prison for the rest of your life for doing things of this kind. You ought to commit suicide. That's what I think of people of this kind. You ought to commit suicide. You are lower than animals and haven't the right to live in organized society.

There is nothing we can do with you. You expect the County to take care of you. Maybe Hitler was right. The animals in our society ought to be destroyed because they have no right to live among human beings. If you refuse to act like a human being, then, you don't belong among the society of human beings.

Mr. Lucero: Your honor, I don't think I can sit here and listen to that sort of thing.

The Court: You are going to have to listen to it because I think this is a very vulgar, rotten human being.

Mr. Lucero: The Court is indicting the whole Mexican group . . . The Court ought to look at this youngster and deal with this youngster's case.

The Court: All right. That's what I'm going to do. The family should be able to control this boy and the young girl.

Mr. Lucero: What appalls me is that the Court was saying that Hitler was right in genocide.

The Court: What are we going to do with the mad dogs of our society? Either we have to kill them or send them to an institution or place them out of the hands of good people because that's the theory—one of the theories of punishment is if they get to the position that they want to act like mad dogs, then we have to separate them from our society.

As Ed Krueger traveled through the valley and into long-established churches, he began asking questions. How does a migrant feel when he has to travel the back roads out of fear? Is he afraid that his old car might break down on our modern superhighways and he will land in jail? How does he feel when he sees signs advertising the host of services and the products of industrial America which he cannot have? How does he feel about a policeman who follows him in the squad car and dogs him from one end of the city to another town so that he is afraid to stop at a drive-in for a Coke or potato chips? How should the migrant regard a gas-station attendant who sells the gas but refuses to let the migrant use his rest rooms or drink his water?

With these thoughts on his mind, Ed Krueger began his work, seeing that his function in the South Texas Valley would best be utilized in his work among the migrant shanty towns and the established churches of the area. He became a part of the Valley Service Committee, especially concerned with the strategic life of the community both among the seasonal farm workers and the low-income families.

Ed soon found himself spending most of his time with the poor. He began organizing seminars and consultations among growers, workers and church leaders to thrash out problems. But Ed's thrust was community organization and the Mexican-American poor. He then found himself in a cross fire between the Texas Establishment, who wanted to distribute Thanksgiving baskets and clothing to the poor, and his personal beliefs that saw the poor moving to better their lot through an action culture.

CHAPTER 2

Out of the cocoon

THE Reverend Theodore Hesburgh, president of Notre Dame University, said, "If you were caught in the web of poor education, lack of economic opportunity, the last hired and the first fired even for menial jobs, poor housing and degraded neighborhoods, shamed a dozen times a day because whatever your quality as a person you could not eat or rest or sleep where others can, if this were your lot, would you cry, 'Freedom now'? And would you consider this impatience if your cry came a hundred years after you had been declared free?"

This statement applies particularly to the civil rights movement, but the details apply to the Mexican-American as well. Freedom is what is sought. In the Rio Grande Valley there has in the past few years been an awakening, a stirring within the cocoon. The illiterate and poverty-plagued migrant workers are breaking out of the bounds of the Cactus Curtain and starting to assert a sense of their own worth and dignity. Their passive outlook on life is turning to activism. They are learning to meet together to discuss their problems.

It began with the United Farm Workers Organizing

Committee, an unusual kind of union, looking at the valley from its headquarters in Delano, California. The fledgling union is the brainchild of Cesar Chavez, a messianic leader, who has emerged from the ranks of the California *campesinos,* and this union is locked in two life-and-death struggles. One is the farm strike in the Rio Grande Valley, in which Ed Krueger has played a significant role, and the other is in the San Joaquin Valley in California.

The need, first of all, is to recognize that there is an agricultural revolution taking place. In the last ten years about 25 per cent of America's small farms have disappeared. In 1910, one out of every three Americans lived on a family farm. Today the 11.5 million people on the nation's farms represent less than 6 per cent of the population.

Farms have become "agribusiness." The owners of the farms live in metropolitan areas, from which they run their giant holdings. These men then extend their influence into all areas of economic life. They are immensely powerful, as they control the land and farm labor wages. Two examples of such holdings in the Rio Grande Valley are La Casita Farms and Trophy Farms. In California, the Kern County Land Company holds 350,000 acres; Southern Pacific Railroad, 200,000 acres; Standard Oil, 218,000 acres; J. G. Boswell holdings, 108,200 acres; Tejon Ranch, controlled by the owners of the Los Angeles *Times,* 168,000 acres; Anderson Clayton, 52,000 acres; DiGiorgio Fruit Corporation, 26,000 acres; and Russell Giffen, 33,000 acres.

These giants are involved in huge financial networks. For example, Hunt Foods, one of California's biggest "farmers" and probably best known for its tomato sauce, turned up in a fight several years ago to control

Crucible Steel. Hunt Foods also was reported to have an important stake in ABC, the McCall Corporation and Canada Dry Corporation.

Therefore, when we talk about cattle, tomatoes, sugar, vegetables, we could also be talking about oil, steel, real estate, gas and communications. What is happening to the farm worker is tied in with interlocking corporations.

In this type of situation agricultural employers have the final decision over working conditions, hiring and firing, Most seasonal farm workers do not have contracts; their annual income is low, and they do not get overtime pay, paid vacations or unemployment insurance. If a worker is told to show up for work at 6 A.M. and the equipment is not ready or the crop is wet and cannot be worked until 10 A.M., he is not paid for those four hours. Workers can be laid off in the middle of the day, in the middle of the week or weeks on end, without an explanation as to when work will be available. Toilets and drinking fountains are missing from the fields. Inhuman speed-ups and abusive supervision are commonplace. Workers are denied the protection of social legislation enjoyed by most American workers, on the grounds that "agriculture is different."

The National Labor Relations Act states that an employer must sit down with, bargain with and discuss grievances with elected representatives of his workers so that they can share in the decisions which crucially affect their lives. Administration is made up of a board of five members appointed by the President. The National Labor Relations Board conducts elections among workers of an employer to determine whether or not the majority wish to have a union represent them in the relationship with the employer.

Employers are forbidden by law to interfere with

workers' organizing efforts, to refuse to bargain in good faith, to discriminate against workers for union activity. They cannot, for example, organize a "company" union or show favoritism toward one union over another; they cannot fire, or refuse to hire, workers for reasons of union membership; they cannot refuse to deal with workers' representatives because the workers are out on strike.

Labor unions are prohibited from engaging in coercion, secondary boycotts, refusing to bargain collectively in good faith or charging excessive union initiation fees.

When the bill was written in 1935, it included farm workers. However, when it was reported out of committee two months later, the farm workers were specifically excluded. Adequate justification for this exclusion was not given. The Senate reported "administrative reasons," and the House reason was just as vague. The bill's sponsor in the House said, ". . . The committee discussed this matter carefully in executive session and decided not to include agricultural workers. We hope that the agricultural workers will be taken care of . . . I am in favor of giving agricultural workers every protection, but just now I believe in biting off one mouthful at a time. If we can get this bill through and get it working properly, there will be opportunity later, and I hope soon, to take care of the agricultural workers."

The act has been amended four times since Congress took that first "bite." After thirty-four years the agricultural worker is still waiting for the bill to work smoothly—for protection?—for opportunity?

Although agriculture is the third most hazardous industry in the nation, workers often lack workmen's compensation. Children of farm workers are not protected—or if so, the laws are unenforced under the Fair Labor Standards Act. Since the income is low, the whole family must work whenever possible. When farm workers have tried to organize themselves, they have not been protected as industrial workers, so they have been subject to refusal, eviction, dismissal and terror.

Suppose that a worker has a complaint; how is it registered? Imagine that you are a sugar-beet worker who wants to complain about wages that are below the minimum established by the U. S. Sugar Act. You go to the county agricultural stabilization and conservation committee for remedial action. The committee is composed of and elected by the growers. They not only administer their own price-support program, but they also police themselves in regard to wages.

Do you want to go to the law about your problem? You will find that the county sheriff, who is responsible for fair and reasonable law enforcement in times of tension such as occur during a strike, works for the county board of supervisors, which in most agricultural counties is composed entirely of agricultural employers. Likewise, the county welfare department, which is to serve poor people in times of need, is also controlled by the board of supervisors. County housing authorities are also under the control of the supervisors.

As a result, farm workers and their families remain poor and have little opportunity to break out of the cycle of poverty which has entrapped them for generations. The social and political forces of the agricultural valleys are controlled by the affluent to serve the needs of affluent men and their children.

CHAPTER 3

The union sows its seeds

"IT IS not what one would call a spectacular entrance to a farm," I remarked to Ed Krueger as we wheeled up to a gate in an old dusty Rambler. There were two long weather-beaten poles on each side of the road, standing high enough for large trucks and buses to get through. Stretching across the road from one pole to the other was an equally weather-beaten sign about a foot wide on which, many years ago to judge by the lettering, had been painted the name of the ranch—La Casita Farms. Staring down the monotonous road that seemed to stretch into infinity, one could see only flat fields planted with melons. It was not an inspiring sight. In contrast to the old signs identifying the farm, new ones had been nailed to the fence in both Mexican and English—"no trespassing," "keep out," "private property." Ed appeared uncomfortable as I took his picture at the gate.

As the eye sweeps around the landscape, the sight is almost forbidding. It is hot, dusty and dry, as the blistering Texas sun beats down on the ground, soon parching and cracking it. Without water, the land would not be worth much. But thanks to federally subsidized dams and irrigation, the scrubland has been turned productive, principally from the Rio Grande River, which flows to the south not far from La Casita. Fifteen years ago there was no La Casita Farms; there were very few jobs, and even a lone cow had a difficult time foraging to fill one stomach.

Following World War II, California farming interests saw the possibilities of raising potatoes, carrots, other vegetables and melons in the Rio Grande Valley. The use of irrigation, the development of refrigeration for trains and trucks made it practical to raise food even though it was a great distance from the markets. Hardin Farms of California, Incorporated, organized a subsidiary in Texas—La Casita—purchased land and began its operations.

But not all was bare land when La Casita and other large farms, such as Trophy Farms, Sun Tex Farms and Starr Farms, came into the area. For many generations the economy of the Rio Grande Valley had been upheld by citrus farming. This kind of farming had its ups and downs. Besides, competition was intense from the citrus groves of Florida and California.

Allan R. Brockway, former editor of the now defunct *Concern* magazine of the United Methodist Church, describes the region as being "socially and politically controlled by *patrons*, through a system that may aptly be compared to medieval feudalism. The families who are now farm workers were little more than serfs of the patrons. That system is far from broken today, as becomes obvious when the centers of wealth and political power are seen to reside with a few farm owners and managers who live comfortably alongside a majority of the population . . ."

Turning our backs to the La Casita main gate, Ed and I went across the road to the little settlement, also called La Casita. Here the houses are mostly made of red brick, now bleached from the hot sun. Ed spoke in Spanish to several women standing nearby. They knew what hard work was—one could see it in their callused and cracked hands and their tanned, prematurely wrinkled faces. Mrs. Juanita Herandez, beautiful despite the ravages of the sun and the long hours of labor, invited us into her modest home; I took a place on a well-worn couch next to Ed. She introduced us to three of her children; she has fourteen in all. A baby, one month old, slept in a small cradle.

She told us about working in the melon fields. "You stoop when you work in the fields. The vines have to be gently placed on top of the furrows so that the water can run between each furrow."

Then she illustrated how the workers straddle the row and walk like waddling ducks, pulling the vines together. "Everybody starts together at the beginning of the furrow, and those who fall behind get a few choice words from the crew boss. Those who are slow are helped by a member of the family working next to them. At the end of the furrow, you can straighten up and get a drink of warm water from a common cup."

"Tell me about picking melons. How do you do it?" I asked, knowing full well that the June sun does not wait for man or melon in the Rio Grande Valley.

"The work is hard," said Mrs. Herandez. "The melons get ripe very quickly, so that you might have to pick a field more than once during a day. You have a canvas bag that hangs from the shoulder with a metal loop around the mouth to keep it open. As you stoop along the furrow, you give the melon a little twist; if it is ripe, it will break loose from the vine. The bag holds about twenty-five melons which weigh a pound each, sometimes more. The strap cuts deeper into your shoulder as the bag starts to fill. Sometimes the skin cracks and bleeds, and you put a rag under the strap so it won't hurt. The pain you get in your neck is unbearable.

"When the bag fills up, you carry it to the truck, not drag it, because that would bruise the fruit. You take big steps over the furrows so you don't disturb the melons which are getting ripe. Sometimes it's a long way to the truck. Once there, you climb up the narrow plank to the bed and gently dump out the melons. That is the best part; you get to rest your shoulder. That feels good."

How much could one person expect to be paid for this work? If a worker is fortunate, he may get $1.25 an hour. More than likely he will get anything from forty cents to a dollar an hour on land where the profits sometimes exceed five hundred dollars an acre. Not only has the pay been poor, but there also is a great deal of pain involved in planting and harvesting. For example, when picking cotton, and some is still done by hand, the small thorns around the cotton boll stab the fingers. Cotton pickers often spend the evening digging the slivers out of their fingers with a small needle. When planting onions the old way, pushing the seed into the ground with the end of a finger, the dirt under the nail separates it from the quick and the finger can become severely swollen by the end of the day. Harvesting the onion is done by clipping the stems near the bulb, causing the wrist to swell and making the thumb feel as if it would tear loose from the hand. Chopping weeds and loosening the soil in the lettuce fields involves the use of hoes with handles a foot long. This means bending over all day. It would be far more comfortable to kneel occasionally, but the crew boss doesn't tolerate this slowdown comfort. He bellows down the rows so everyone gets the message, "Get off your knees. Go to church if you want to pray. Get to work!"

There is always the drifting pesticide from the crop duster. The bug-killing dust, delivered by plane or mechanical ground monsters, leaves field workers and villages like La Casita located on the edges of the fields choking and gasping for pure air.

Pesticides are a real nemesis to the farm worker. Francisco Mendoza said in court, "Every summer when I'm involved in the harvest, I get sick due to the pesticides. I get pains in my stomach, I throw up and I get headaches. Sometimes I get chills and have itching sensations over my entire body. My eyesight has been steadily getting worse, but when I work in the field, my vision gets very bad."

There is no doubt that birds and bees are dying at an alarming rate from pesticides, and clinics set up in areas where there are farm workers have revealed that the problem is serious for humans and animals as well. Pesticide companies have refused to divulge how and where their products are used. The problem is that the workers do not know how dangerous the dust is. They call it dust or spray, but those "in the know" refer to it as poison. Often the diseases resulting from pesticides are subtle. The worker does not know what is happening to him until it is too late. Many of the workers fail to report cases of poisoning, as they mistake their ailments for other illnesses.

C. Seldon Morely, agricultural commissioner in California's Kern County, thinks the farm worker has exaggerated the harm of pesticides. "Agricultural pesticides and chemicals are a way of American life today," said the commissioner. "If it weren't for pesticides we would be having a lot of worms in our apples and everything else."

Jerome Cohen, general counsel for farm workers, said one day after passing a row of billboards advertising pesticides, "The growers care more about bugs and weeds than about their workers."

No one paid much attention to the plight of the Mexican-American farm worker in the Rio Grande Valley as he burned or poisoned himself out at an early age. That is, not until 1966, when a young man named Eugene Nelson, trained in Delano, California, moved into the Texas Valley and saw the opportunity to organize the farm workers into a union to demand higher wages. Gene was not an official organizer but wanted to do something on his own. So he began by making speeches, soliciting aid from the Texas Council of Churches and other interested groups. Rallies were held in communities such as Rio Grande City, the county seat of Starr County, which a Texan described as having "a curiously shrunken look, like a man whose clothes are too big, as if it was built with more people and more activity in mind and neither materialized. Its streets are often empty, its stores quiet, their keepers somnolent."

Some of the towns, like Roma, still look like Mexican villages did fifty years ago. At a Rio Grande City rally in San Juan Plaza, Gene said, "You must be brave . . . You are the sons of Zapata . . . in the traditions of the Mexican and American revolutions, and as citizens of the United States, you should stand up for your rights."

Gene Nelson, who had served as a strike captain in Delano, had come to Texas primarily to organize the boycott against Schenley products and thought the farm workers in the Rio Grande Valley were ready to organize. News of successes in California encouraged the workers so that by the end of May 1966, Nelson had signed up seven hundred workers and announced the formation of the Independent Workers' Association.

On June 1, 1966, a strike was called and pickets appeared at three of the larger melon farms and five packing sheds. The workers asked for $1.25 an hour and a union contract between growers and the union. Within twenty-four hours the growers had obtained a temporary restraining order prohibiting pickets at the farms initially struck. Picketing was continued at other farms, and the strike idea was kept alive by local marches and rallies. The growers sent trucks to the border bridge to pick up the "green-card" and Mexican workers used as strikebreakers. Daily the pickets were there to dissuade the Mexicans.

Much has been written about the green carders, who actually carry a blue card. They are Mexican nationals legally admitted to work in this country as permanent residents. Prior to July 1, 1963, such status was gained by proof that the applicant would not become a public charge. This meant, in most cases, the endorsement by a financially solvent relative or friend in the United States and a certified promise of employment plus the necessary credentials.

Since July 1, 1963, an important procedural limitation was introduced by the U. S. Department of Labor, applicable only to Mexican nationals but not to would-be immigrants of other nationalities. In essence, the limitation enables the Department of Labor, through its affiliated state employment agencies, to rule whether employment of the alien would adversely affect the wages and working conditions of domestic workers. This cut the number of green carders from 55,253 in 1963 to 32,967 in 1964.

A green carder is under no obligation to establish residence anywhere in the United States so long as he complies with the minimum requirement of at least one day's work north of the Rio Grande every six months. If he so desires, he may establish residence. A large number of Mexicans elect to commute between Mexico and north of the Rio Grande. It is hard to tell how many bona fide legal residents of the United States and commuters come across the border. On one January day, in the low month of the agricultural season, there were 20,234 green-card commuters in Texas, 16,609 in California, 5,591 in Arizona and 17 in New Mexico for a total of 42,451.

Until October 11, 1968, "wetbacks," Mexicans who illegally enter the United States by swimming across the Rio Grande River, were entering the country in a rising flood. In the month of September, border patrolmen of the U. S. Immigration and Naturalization Service seized more than fourteen thousand of them, one thousand more than the monthly average. Thousands more filter past roadblocks and airplane spotters or wade through the shallow waters of the Rio Grande River as they search for jobs as "stoop laborers" on the nearby farms. Most of the wetbacks cross the border on their own, while at the same time illegal labor contractors smuggle others across.

The traffic keeps the border patrols busy all the way from Brownsville, Texas, to Chula Vista, California. One day in San Antonio two camper trucks were stopped and fifteen wetbacks were found in one and seventeen in the other. They were escorted back to the border in the anticipation that they would stay on the Mexican side. However, many returned to become the special curse of the United Farm Workers Organizing Committee (UFWOC:CIO-AFL), which has tried to wage an uphill battle against the wetbacks in an effort to organize the migrant American farm workers. In the Rio Grande

valley, farmers attempting to break the 1966 strike hired
the illegal workers to harvest the five-million-dollar crop
of melons. In the first six months of 1968 some 2200
wetbacks were arrested in Kern County, California,
where Cesar Chavez is trying to organize the grape
workers.

In May 1968, I made an attempt to photograph the
green carders as they poured across the border at the
Reynosa International Bridge at 6:15 A.M. An immigration and naturalization officer threatened to seize my
camera. Even though a sign of photograph regulations
is posted at the gate, he ordered me to move on, contending that I was violating security regulations and subject
to arrest. I took the pictures anyhow.

In early 1969 Narciso Aleman was not as fortunate with
his camera as I had been. His experience shows the contempt of whites toward Mexican-Americans. He had
gone to the Texas Employment Commission to inquire
about a job. He was told to go to Reynosa Bridge because
that is where farm workers are hired. Trucks and buses
with the crew chiefs wait there for the green carders to
come across the border. Narciso and Marcos Lopez from
McAllen, Texas, arrived at the bridge at 5 A.M. Marcos
drove around through the crowd slowly while Narciso
took pictures from the car of green-card farm workers
boarding a bus. The observers parked the car, got out
and took some more photos and then walked over to the
checkpoint at the bridge.

From outside the building through a glass wall, Narciso
snapped a picture of the steady flow of people from Mexico, all dressed as farm workers. "Immediately," said Narciso, "all three immigration officers surrounded me and
demanded the film."

When he offered to send the officers a copy of the

prints, he was ordered to expose his film. When he refused, he was taken into the building while the officers said, "We will call Mr. Snowball, our boss."

Then one of the American officers asked, "Who are you and what are you doing here?"

Narciso explained, "I am working for the National Student Association, and we were conducting an economic study of the area to learn what effect the influx of green carders has upon the citizens of the Rio Grande Valley and how this affected the educational level of Mexican-American students." The officer seemed unimpressed. He asked for identification papers.

Then he said, "You have violated a federal regulation that prohibits taking pictures on federal property." (How many people break this law every day when they take photographs in parks, at military installations, in Washington, D.C., and in the federal areas that are strategic defense areas?)

When Narciso asked to be shown the federal regulation under which he was being detained, the officer responded with, "I don't have to." He then took the camera, asked that it be left until 8 AM. when the boss would arrive and continued to threaten Narciso with arrest.

What followed resembled a nightmare. "After what seemed like a long time, the two officers questioning me said they had called the city marshal. I was too scared to think of measuring the time that I had been interrogated at the checkpoint or to get the officer's name or even to think that I was on federal property and that the Hidalgo, Texas, city marshal had no jurisdiction on federal property; therefore, he could not legally arrest me. I tried to determine for sure what I was being arrested for, but all they kept saying was for taking pictures on federal property. I said I needed to know so I could notify my attorney, but the city marshal said, 'You do that later; right now you come with me.'

"One of the officers signed a form but did not fill in the charge. At this point the marshal took me by the arm and led me to his car. In the car I tried to explain what I was doing and who I worked for, but he just kept saying I was being detained. It was not until two hours later that I was able to talk to the judge. She told me there was no regulation (except in certain places involving security) about not taking photographs at the checkpoint and I was free to go. After all of that fear and discomfort, there was no law that I had violated. Because three federal employees at the immigration checkpoint had invented a law, I went through all that hell."

When Narciso went back for his camera and had the film developed, he found that it had been exposed.

This is the kind of harassment that plagues those who try to take pictures of green carders in the valley.

Forging the green cards has become a business along border bridges. The going price for a forged green card, the union says, is $150.

The added influx of wetbacks coincided with moves in 1968 to restrict legal entry of migrant workers. Former Secretary of Labor Willard Wirtz halted the flow of workers from Mexico, who came into this country at the rate of four hundred thousand a year. These workers, said Wirtz, were no longer needed. The union organizers welcomed the move, but, said Cesar Chavez, dynamic leader of the California grape boycott, "The *braceros* have become dispensable primarily because the U. S. Government, bowing to the growers' wishes, is so lax in its vigilance of the 2013-mile border that thousands of Mexican laborers cross into the United States illegally."

Called well after the melon season had gotten under

way, the 1966 strike had little effect on the growers because of the steady stream of green carders and wetbacks.
Nature herself entered the picture—storms lashed into the
Rio Grande Valley and south Texas, inundating the
countryside. Tens of thousands were left homeless, and
valuable winter crops were wiped out, along with jobs
for the already destitute Mexican-American workers.

The drive to organize the farm workers was a failure.
The part labor union, part civil rights campaign, part
religious crusade and spin-off of Cesar Chavez's California grape-strike movement (to be discussed in another
chapter) had suffered a temporary setback. However, it
produced one of the most dramatic demonstrations ever
held by Texas agricultural workers.

After the aborted strike, the workers decided to make
a pilgrimage march as had been done in California
when grape workers marched from Delano to Sacramento, dramatizing to the state and nation the conditions and wages that farm workers had to endure. As the
Texas march, called *La Marcha* by its participants,
wound through the southern part of the state, thousands
of farm workers joined in for a mile, a day or a week.
Bishop Humberto Medeiros greeted the workers in San
Juan and held a special Mass for them at the shrine there.
He endorsed the strikers' demands and defined their right
to organize into a union. Then the marchers set out for
Corpus Christi, San Antonio and Austin, the state capital.
Supported by sympathetic citizens at each stop, the
workers found shelter and food at Protestant and Catholic churches, in parks and beside the road. *La Marcha*
ended on Labor Day 1966. Over fifteen thousand people
joined in the final day. Among those were the leaders of
the AFL-CIO and unions throughout the state and nation
—Domingo Arrendondo, the strike chairman and head of

the Starr County farm workers, Eugene Nelson, Cesar Chavez, and Bill Kircher, head of the organizing department of the AFL-CIO.

A Catholic priest, Father Antonio Gonzales, and a Baptist minister from Houston, the Reverend James L. Navarro, had served as co-ordinators of the march. Seventy-four marchers had started out on July 4, and twenty-five made the entire trip in the continuing demonstration.

Sixty-two-year-old Reyes Alaniz marched all the way. "I am doing it with my own heart," he said in Austin. "I have already wasted all my life in the fields . . . I passed the hard way. I don't want the new generation to struggle like I did."

On August 27, just before the march reached the capital, San Antonio's archbishop, the Most Reverend Robert Emmet Lucey, endorsed the minimum-wage demands in a Mass. He said, "No sane man would consider that a fair wage these days . . . we join you . . . only because you have known the sorrow of cruel wages in the past and this objective is a step in the right direction . . . A wage of $1.25 an hour is ghastly recompense for exhausting labor under the burning sun of Texas."

Senator Ralph Yarborough joined the marchers on the final day and was the key speaker at the Labor Day rally. He endorsed the $1.25 demand. The governor had met the marchers five days before they reached the capital but was not present when they arrived. It was reported that he had gone dove hunting. He disapproved of the march and did not call a special session of the legislature to consider the minimum-wage demands. Signs carried at the rally said, "Remember, we can vote," and "Search your soul, Governor; this is the 20th century."

The strike was a failure in one sense. It did not win

contracts or the passage of the $1.25 minimum wage. But in another sense, it was just the beginning. It did end forever the myth that Mexican-Americans are happy, contented, satisfied with second-class citizenship and a life of poverty. It awakened the youth.

As editor David M. Fishlow of *Zapata,* the Texas UFWOC, AFL-CIO, paper, wrote, "The political fall upsets showed that Mexican-Americans would no longer blindly accept a corrupt political machine that opposed their interests. Thousands of workers began organizing and joining unions throughout the state, and the whole labor movement was the beneficiary of this new spirit. *La Marcha* was symbolic of and contributed to the ever-quickening awakening of the Mexican-Americans in Texas. It was symbolic of the end of an era. But the hard task of organizing farm workers and building a democratic union and a new order of justice lay ahead."

CHAPTER 4

Texas Valley influenced by Cesar Chavez

IN AN AD appearing in several national magazines there was a statement that "John and Mary Bodkin of Detroit, Michigan, plunk down $195 in the supermarket every month." To maintain a decent standard of living, this naval architect and his wife need to spend this much on everything from detergents to frozen crepes.

But what about the farm worker? How much of the male worker's approximately two thousand dollars per year can he "plunk down" in the supermarket? How about the family with an income of 2500 to 3000 dollars? Was a union the way to bring the good things of life to the tables of the poor?

I talked with Ed Krueger about this, and he was concerned. But he was careful to point out that "I have not in the past nor am I at present engaged in getting people to join unions. Union activity is not the role of the valley ministry."

Yet as the talk about unions waxed hot and heavy in the cities and colonies along the Rio Grande, there was an eager word from California. The history of the labor movement there is integrally intermeshed not only with south Texas but also with land all along the Mexican border states. Ed Krueger had told me that he had a great deal of respect for one man who had become the hero of Mexican-Americans—Cesar Chavez.

At Ed's suggestion, I left the Rio Grande valley and went out to California to meet Chavez.

On September 8, 1965, several hundred Filipino farm workers went on strike to better their lot against their grape-grower employers in and around Delano, which is located about thirty miles north of Bakersfield in the rich San Joaquin Valley of California. On September 20 they were joined by over a thousand Mexican-American farm workers under the leadership of Cesar Chavez, sometimes called the Reuther of the farm industry and the Bolívar of the migratory worker, and his National Farm Workers Association (NFWA).

Cesar, whose father had come from Mexico, was born on his grandfather's farm in Yuma, Arizona, one of six children. During the Depression the farm was foreclosed. The family migrated to California and started moving with the crops. Chavez first worked in Delano when he was ten. He recalls how he had to walk to school barefoot through the mud because the family was so poor. When school was over, "we fished in the canal and cut wild-mustard greens—otherwise we would have had nothing to eat."

In describing some of his early experiences, he said, "Everyone else left the Arizona camp we were in, but we did not have the money even to do that. Finally, some of our relatives sent us a few dollars, so we bought enough gas for our Studebaker to get up to Los Angeles. In L.A. my mother sold crocheting to get us to Brawley. We lived in our car for three days before we found a place to rent. The next winter we were stranded in Oxnard and had to spend the winter in a tent. We went to bed as soon as the sun went down because there was no light. In the morning my mother and father left before sunrise to go to the farms to pick peas. They would tell us that it cost seventy-five cents to go to the fields in a truck, so some days they did not even make enough money to pay for their transportation. To help out, my brother and I collected tin foil from empty cigarette packages that we found along the streets. We made a huge ball which we sold to a junk dealer and bought ourselves tennis shoes and two sweat shirts."

Chavez finished the eighth grade, attending a total of thirty-seven schools. "I went to some of them for only two or three days before the family was on the move again."

He recalls the lowest wage that he ever was paid. "It was twelve and a half cents an hour. We were thinning cantaloupes in Imperial Valley. That was in 1941." The family eventually settled in a slum near San Jose called by its inhabitants "Sal Si Puedes" (Get out if you can).

Cesar at the age of nineteen entered the Navy in 1944 and served in the Pacific for two years. He returned to Delano, where he married Helen Fabela. They both did farm work for several years until in 1951 Cesar was discovered by Fred Ross, who at the time was building a militant grass-roots Mexican-American organization under the sponsorship of the Industrial Areas Foundation (IAF). The organization was called the Community Service Organization (CSO) and offered Mexican-Americans legal assistance and advice on citizenship among other things. The CSO was founded in East Los Angeles in 1949 and received much of its impetus from a victory over Chief of Police William H. Parker in a case of alleged police brutality. The possibility of effective action against police harassment attracted Chavez and a number of other ex-GI militants in San Jose. Eventually, Chavez became the national director of the CSO and continued working for ten years with Fred Ross in developing chapters throughout California and even in Arizona. The CSO thus became the most powerful voice representing Mexican-Americans in the Southwest.

Like many other Mexican-American farm workers, Chavez encountered both discrimination and abject poverty. He was once arrested in Delano while sitting with his wife in the theater—he had refused to comply with the theater's policy of seating Mexican-Americans on one side, Anglos on the other.

In April of 1962, Chavez was convinced that farm labor organizing was the primary need of the Mexican-American people. He was also convinced that CSO would not or could not take on the task. "I had some ideas on what should be done," he said. "No great plans, just that it would take an awful lot of work to organize farm workers. It was a gamble. I went around for about eleven months and visited over eighty communities and labor camps. I found people who were committed to doing something. They were ready for a change."

Chavez left his paid position with CSO and moved into a faded two-bedroom frame house with his wife and eight children in Delano, his wife's birthplace and the winter home for many years of his own family. His purpose was to begin building a militant and democratic farm workers' union that would be composed of farm workers, paid for by farm workers and run by farm workers. He traveled to each farming community in the San Joaquin Valley, seeking out those who would be willing to sacrifice and pay the price. He promised nothing but hard work and risks. Those that were not willing to endure for the cause were not intimidated; they were passed up. Cesar levied a

monthly due of $3.50 as a test of intention. He himself
worked without any salary. He and his family went to the
fields, keeping in mind that he wanted to build a farm
workers' organization that would be independent, financially free—a group that would make the decisions that
affected their own lives. They eventually developed a
credit union, a store, a newspaper and a health clinic.

Chavez's organization was called the National Farm
Workers Association. During the summer of 1965 his group
and another, the Agricultural Workers Organizing Committee (AFL-CIO), were organizing the grape pickers
around Delano. The prevailing wage was $1.15 an hour.
On September 8, the AWOC, mostly Filipinos, struck, de-
manding a minimum wage of $1.40. The growers made
no response to the demand for the wage increase. Thirty-
four ranches were affected. In addition to higher wages,
there was a demand for improved working conditions and
later a union contract. On one farm in the Delano area,
sixty-seven workers had to drink water from a single
empty beer can. Lacking state-required portable toilets,
the workers had to relieve themselves in the fields. Eight
days later, Chavez's union joined the strike. He had hesi-
tated, fearing that the NFWA was not ready for such a
crucial undertaking, but within a few days he realized
that this strike of fellow workers had to be supported.
Later, in August 1966, the two groups merged and became the United Farm Workers Organizing Committee,
AFL-CIO. Chavez was named director with a joint committee to command. "*Huelga*" (strike) became the workers' rallying cry.

Only the largest ranches were struck: Schenley, the
Sierra Vista Ranch of DiGiorgio and others that employed
thousands. The growers responded as the farm workers
had expected—they returned union letters unopened,

hired strikebreakers, denied the existence of the strike and harassed pickets. When strikers were seen coming down the road, workers were moved from along the road to the middle of the field, out of earshot of bullhorns and loudspeakers. Other growers would drive along the edge of their property with tractors and choke the strikers with dust, while still others would direct spraying machines toward the strikers, covering them with insecticide and fertilizer. Picket signs were taken from the strikers and riddled with bullets. The strikers were tripped and elbowed. Injunctions to limit picketing were secured, and groups were arrested for unlawful assembly.

In some cases, the police seemed to go out of their way to harass the roving pickets. As one complained that the police would stop him to check his lights, others told how they were detained for failure to indicate a turn or were told that the muffler was too loud. The police had cameras and tape recorders with them. Visitors to Delano were followed by police. Even when I drove into town, a police car followed me up to the home of Jim and Susan Drake, closely associated administratively with Chavez and the California Migrant Ministry.

In a case often repeated at union headquarters, pickets were threatened by workers still in the fields. Instead of arresting the workers making the threats, the Kern County Sheriff's Office once arrested the pickets. When the Senate Subcommittee on Migratory Labor held meetings in Delano, the late Robert Kennedy confronted Roy Galyen, the Kern County sheriff:

Kennedy: What did you charge them with?

Galyen: Violation of—unlawful assembly.

Kennedy: I think that is most interesting. Who told you they were going to riot?

Galyen: The men right out in the field that they were

talking to said, "If you don't get them out of here, we're going to cut their hearts out." So rather than let them get cut, we removed the cause.

Kennedy: This is a most interesting concept, I think. How can you arrest somebody if they haven't violated the law?

Galyen: They're ready to violate the law.

Kennedy: Can I suggest that the sheriff read the Constitution of the United States?

Chavez could no longer keep from becoming deeply involved in the strike. He made speeches in public, usually wearing cotton slacks and an open-necked shirt, and worked diligently to gather support for the grape pickers. The strike in its infancy and thereafter was marred by bitterness and acts of violence. Four attempts were made to burn the union hall in Delano. A co-operative gas station owned by the farm workers was bombed. One grower sued Chavez for libel, seeking six million dollars in damages. The suit was later dropped when the union settled its dispute with the company. Chavez in 1966 was arrested for trespassing on the DiGiorgio Corporation farm and fined $276.

Throughout the strike there has been urging by some of the active young militants to resort to violence. Chavez has called for peace and reason. In a two-hour interview that I had with him in the bedroom of his very modest home in February 1969, he emphasized the need for communication and nonviolence. Sometimes he cannot hold his followers back. No one knows for sure who did it, but piles of packing boxes have been put to the torch. Rocks have been thrown through windows of strikebreakers' homes and signs set up on lawns: "A Scab Lives Here."

But Chavez is determined to keep the farm movement

nonviolent. He does not want his followers to "lose their cool," to precipitate irrational behavior. He goes out and sees to it that bloodshed is averted. "No union movement is worth the life of a single grower or his child, or the life of a single worker or his child," he has preached repeatedly.

When I spoke to Chavez, he had slowed down considerably from his earlier years. The stoop labor of his teens had begun to tell on him; he was in pain from a spinal ailment. He goes swimming every day in a heated pool belonging to a friend, and his followers are constantly about to see that he takes his pills on schedule. As a matter of fact, some co-workers are always around the house, for there have been threats on Chavez's life. A new addition to the family is a police dog behind the white picket fence of the modest dwelling.

Cesar is a short man (five feet six inches) with a dark brown complexion, jet black hair and restless, sad eyes. He shows traces of his Indian ancestry. His voice is soft, unassuming, pleasantly accented and perfectly modulated. As his aides come into the room, one can sense a quiet power which burns with a consuming desire to lift the lot of his people. Even while we talked, he carried on his business from his bed; he signed checks, asked questions, prepared for communications, listened to the problems of the strikers and welcomed his brother, who had just returned from a long automobile ride. The night before I saw him, Cesar had been at the union hall talking to farm workers. The next day he was reaping the rewards —uncomfortable back pain. In the past, if I had wanted to talk to Chavez, I would have had to move with him. Usually conversation could best be gained by volunteering to be his chauffeur, for he does not have a car. Those who know him best say that he transacts most of his

business from the front seat of an automobile as he trav-
els from one locality to another.

In talking with several of his aides, Chavez said that
everything for 1969 was to be geared to sacrifice. "We
will have a small crew who are going to work for
organizing the workers for the rest of their lives." They
are not going to be comfortable, for "social change does
not come easily. From now on," he emphasized, "our men
are going to keep in action. The organizers are going to
stay in cars, not in motels. Not everybody is going to
give up their work, but all of us involved in this strike
are going to have a single purpose to show the world
that farm workers are not happy living the way they are
and that the poor must be mobilized."

In the spring of 1969 Chavez was treated by the same
physician who had helped the late President Kennedy.
Sometimes, however, Chavez throws caution and doctors'
orders to the winds and gets out of his bed to address his
followers, usually at the Filipino Hall. He said, "Now,
more than ever, we are convinced that until the poor are
organized into strong unions, responsive to their members,
our American ideal of equality will only be an empty
dream. Until recently we were not certain that the
achievement of our goals was even possible. Now we view
it as inevitable. But not unless we make demands on ourselves that we have never made before. Not unless each
one of us has the courage to ask himself, 'What can I do?'
and then goes to do it."

Chavez has been aware that his movement could become scholarly and be taken over by the intellectuals.
He is suspicious of the educated Establishment. "If you
want social change, you have to give up your pay check
and make the sacrifice. This is where it counts and
hurts. Lectures and seminars—they are nice, but people

listen and don't do anything. Our people are not afraid of sacrifice; this is our tradition. *Capricho!* We are going to work among the poor. Our spirit is great!"

I asked him what he thinks about being called an outside agitator, a socialist or even a Communist. "I am not a Communist," he answered sharply. "I am a Christian and proud of it. Why is it that if a barber, butcher or baker desires to get ahead and buys himself a piece of land, everyone applauds and admires him. But let a Mexican-American desire a little land and everyone calls him a Communist dupe or worse."

The Delano strike has been difficult yet successful to a degree. Cesar explained what has made it so. "First, the concept of a union for farm workers is like an idea whose time for birth has come. The hour is here. We can never be so bold as to think that it was merely 'our' strategy that has brought some contracts already into being. It was that plus the years of suffering, planning, organizing, striking and learning which went before.

"Second, it cannot be emphasized too often that there is a basic maxim which must apply wherever success is to occur: You cannot organize and strike at the same time. The powers are too great on the side of the opposition; in California, for example, we found that the grower was but a small part of the opposition, for beside him stood the bankers, politicians, Birchers and progrower unions." The same has been true in Texas.

"Third, due to the fact that the farm worker is excluded from the basic protective legislation, a strong, broad coalition of forces must be available, willing to carry their full weight into the battle. We have found that in lieu of elections and democratic procedures for getting labor and management together, sheer economic pressure must be employed. The best weapon yet devised is the boycott, and the boycott means coalesced public power. A simple rule that we follow is: 'Don't be too proud to ask for help.' We have been helped. Young people have come from campuses all over the country, churches have helped and so have political organizations and minority groups.

"Finally, the nature of the union which we are building is of great importance. We are not interested in gloating and letting the world know that 'We have won! We have won!' We are not interested in beating our chest in public. We are not interested in a neat business operation with no heart, for then the workers will scoff, they will turn us down cold. Farm workers have seen too much of that kind of unionism. The union that we are seeking to build is one which guarantees new life. Co-operatives, credit unions, educational programs of a practical nature, money-saving devices . . . these are the elements that are going to go into our farm workers' union. These capture our imaginations. This union must be grass roots with a vengeance. Workers are going to have to learn to do everything for themselves. The most mundane office work to the most sophisticated bargaining must be so divided into steps that farm workers can easily learn and understand them. They will then feel they are a part of all operations of their union."

Cesar Chavez is in the midst of a struggle to win a fair standard of living and the right to collective-bargaining status for the workers in the grape-growing industry as well as in other areas where farm workers have been slaving to bring food to the tables of America. The days have been fraught with struggle.

Cesar Chavez is succeeding where others have failed, because he is a charismatic leader who has capitalized on the ethnic bonds among the Mexican-Americans. His cause has been invested with overtones of religion and civil rights. Said one of the growers, "Chavez's secret is that he has the utter loyalty of the Mexican-American workers. His appeal is primarily racial—and to some extent religious. They are a racial and religious organization." This is a far cry from earlier grower epitaphs, such as "a dumb Mex . . . revolutionary . . . political opportunist . . . Trotskyite."

Another reason for Chavez's success is his patience and diligence. Said an enthusiast, "He burns with a patient fire, poor like us, dark like us." He has carefully laid the groundwork in the past and knows exactly what he is going to do in the future. "A big job has to be done and we know it," he said. "It will take many years. But we know that a union of farm workers is going to be built somehow because the workers are on the move and they want a union."

CHAPTER 5

The wrath of grapes

WHILE in California, I learned that strikes in the rich Imperial Valley are not new. Most of them had been unsuccessful, so the attention of the workers had turned toward voter registration in order to mold groups who could challenge those in political power and in turn shave the dominance of growers. As more migrants moved into the state, this approach became more feasible.

By the years 1964 and 1965 a number of events in the nation's life changed the whole picture for the farm workers. One was the awareness of the nation regarding poverty. Photos and stories began appearing in national magazines. Demands were made on the government to help combat poverty, while at the same time projects were encouraged so that the poor could find jobs. Another stimulus to change was the successful militancy of the civil rights movement. Here again the picture was dramatically brought before the American public by the various communication media, including television. Viewers could see what was taking place as they sat in their living rooms. Still a third impetus was the success

of a long campaign to end the importation of Mexican contract workers.

Deprived of cheap labor, growers turned to other channels. The U. S. Department of Labor had set criteria by
which the grower had to prove a labor shortage before
foreign labor could be imported.

In 1965 the Filipino grape thinners walked out in a demand for higher wages. They were mostly members of the
Agricultural Workers Organizing Committee (AWOC).
The walkout spread north from the Coachella Valley. The
union was asking an increase of from $1.20 to $1.40 an
hour and the raise of piece-work incentive from fifteen to
twenty-five cents per box of grapes. When the strikers
moved into Delano for the second grape harvest, the
wages offered were $1.20 plus ten cents a box. So the
Coachella demands were renewed. The independent
National Farm Workers Association joined the strike and
merged into the United Farm Workers Organizing Committee (UFWOC).

One must remember in this farm labor struggle just
how much each taxpayer is involved in the agricultural
industry. Agribusiness to a large extent owes its life to
federally financed irrigation systems. For example, it was
DiGiorgio, a Sicilian immigrant with vineyard experience
in the old country, who first started vines in the sage-
brush area of the San Joaquin Valley, about 130 miles
northwest of Los Angeles. As the grapes grew, the water
table dropped steadily until the expense of drilling wells
became prohibitive except for the largest operators. The
grape industry was rescued by the Friant-Kern Canal of
the Central Valley's Project of the Federal Bureau of
Reclamation, and the cost of supplying the water is now
estimated at about seven hundred dollars an acre.
Growers pay $123, and the rest is borne by taxpayers and

users of the project electric power. The 160-acres-per-owner limitation on land irrigated by federal water projects, which is supposed to benefit family farmers and not just giant corporations, has been so loosely enforced that DiGiorgio still owns 4600 acres and Schenley 3500.

Cesar Chavez was caught up in the whirlwind of the valley. The strike was on and picket lines were established. They demanded more than just the base pay—everything else had to be negotiated and put into writing. The primary objective was to share in the decisions that affected their lives. Chavez knew that he could not do it alone. There were five thousand vineyard workers in the area and probably no more than three hundred families in his association, and some six hundred to eight hundred in the AWOC under the direction of Larry Itliong. So manpower-wise the strike was almost surely headed for defeat. Besides, growers seemed to find a steady stream of migrants who replaced the workers as soon as they walked off their jobs. Chavez knew that financing, pressures and manpower had to come from the outside. With the proper timing, he sought and won the support of unions, minority groups, antipoverty organizations, student political leaders, clergymen, liberals and radicals.

At this point, before the strike progressed any further, could a new set of circumstances have arisen? Suppose that the growers had given the fifteen-cent-an-hour increase. Would that have ended things for Chavez? Were the growers unnecessarily concerned about weakening the incentive of grape pickers to go all out for piece-rate bonuses?

One grower reminisced, "God, we were plain dumb and out of our minds. We should have held an election right then, and Chavez would not have had a chance. No one had heard of him. He did not have publicity. We would have been the good guys for holding the election, and Chavez would not have been heard from again."

Why had the growers misplayed their cards? Hindsight is always easy, and even one unaccustomed to the game can quarterback on Monday, but could the growers' ills be laid to their greed? They were afraid that one of them might get an advantage or that their profits would be cut.

So the strike was on. *"Huelga"* became the agricultural workers' rallying cry. Buttons and flags began to appear, bearing the picture of the black thunderbird (for sorrow) on a red background (for blood). The farm workers' struggle for a share of the good life became a cause. The American concern for the underdog began to manifest itself in hundreds of ways. Outsiders from all over the country flocked to the valley with food, money, picket signs and clothing. The religious overtones and the involvement of the church (to be more fully covered in the next chapter) brought Catholics, Protestants and Jews to Delano. Said a clergyman, "I'm here because this is a movement by the poor people themselves to improve their status in life. And where the poor are, there should we be also. This is biblical." As in the Bible, the religious and the not-so-religious joined the struggle because it was a battle against the power structure.

How were outsiders welcomed in Delano? With open arms? Far from it! The townspeople raged at the volunteers. Choice words that made the clergy cringe were hurled by passers-by. Most people called the whole thing meddling in local affairs. Students or adults with beards were the butt of vituperative comments. The growers, who run the local churches, politicians and commercial establishments, could not understand what the fuss was all about. "There is no problem here . . . no wage problem.

The farm workers don't want a union; we pay them more now than the union is asking."

In May and June of 1967, UFWOC carried on an organizing campaign among the workers of Giumarra Vineyards Corporation, which owns over twelve thousand acres, half planted in table grapes. According to the union, a registered letter was sent to the company asking for representation elections. The company did not respond. The union then sent a telegram, asking the state conciliation service to arrange a meeting, and through outside efforts tried to arrange a meeting. The company refused. All that was asked at this point was a meeting to discuss fair procedures for a secret ballot that would determine the will of the workers.

But Joe Giumarra was not going to be brought into the fold as was the DiGiorgio Corporation and Schenley and other smaller growers, such as the Christian Brothers, who produce the wine grapes. Joe Giumarra is sixty-nine and tough, perhaps epitomizing the California grape growers. He is an immigrant, proud, independent and one who still works a full day in his vineyards. He came to the United States from southern Europe in the early 1920s, saved his money, lived frugally, bought inexpensive parcels of land and then hit it big when subsidized water began flowing among his grapes.

While some strikers see nothing exemplary about the grape grower, others claim that not all the growers are the "sons-of-bitches" they are made out to be. Rather, they are just unaware and perplexed about what is happening among their rows of grapes and beyond the vineyards. As patrons, the growers feel that what the farm worker wants is what they are willing to give him plus a chance to work hard.

Joe Giumarra doesn't have much to say to interviewers,

but his nephew, John Giumarra, Jr., a graduate of Stanford Law School, is an articulate grower spokesman. He tells how Joe, his three uncles and father came from Sicily, opened a small fruit stand in Los Angeles during the Depression and struggled through those early years. The family now has grown to eleven, with some fifty people who all work on the farm. John, Jr., claims the margin of profit on grapes is low and the weather such a factor that some years can be bad. Even so, he says, the Giumarra Corporation is willing to bargain with a responsible union, but Chavez's group does not fill the bill. Anyway, John Giumarra, Jr., feels that the vineyard workers do not need a union. Like so many growers, he believes that California farm workers have all kinds of opportunities to make over two dollars an hour. Besides, the corporation cannot afford a union. "It's competition. The other states don't pay farm workers like we do . . . a union could drive the pay out of line—the price too." He scoffs at reports of the Labor Department that show labor costs at only two to five cents of every dollar spent by growers and that doubling wages would add only a few cents to the price of a pound of grapes.

The Giumarras and the union could not get together, so Chavez used the same tactic that he used against Schenley—the boycott. In that situation a nationwide boycott was brought against the liquors of Schenley and the canned goods of DiGiorgio, which at the time included S&W Foods. As a high-ranking officer of Schenley said, "We did not go to the bargaining table because of the strike. We were afraid of the adverse effect of the publicity on our products."

It is claimed through the valley that to help minimize the boycott on Giumarra, other growers loaned their labels to the struck grower. By the end of the season, it is said, Giumarra was marketing grapes under his own labels plus one hundred others. So the union had to go all out and boycott the small landowners who are most likely to be hurt by such action. Most farm workers have considerable empathy for the small grower, many of whom are under heavy pressure from the magnates. But the workers are saying to these farmers, "We will not tolerate any longer a situation where your survival in business is purchased by our poverty and the poverty of our children."

Even the hard-pressed small farmer is not in the same economic position as the worker. The farm worker's seasonal employment brings his yearly average wage down to about $2034 a year. The small farmer owns land and can sell it. He has credit at the bank and a place in the community. His child, as one principal put it, "marches to the head of the line because one day he will have to handle the Mexicans," and can look forward to college. The grower has a part in the life of the community and its decisions. Therefore, the farm workers, while sympathetic, are not crying about the squeeze put on the "little growers."

The boycott has had all kinds of ramifications. It has assumed, as Cesar Chavez told me, international proportions. "We are going to extend the boycott into Canada and into Europe. Several Scandinavian countries have refused to import table grapes. That is because we are friendly with several foreign labor unions, and they will help us in the Common Market countries." Such groups as the Canadian Labor Congress have pledged to withhold patronage from California table grapes.

In the large cities of New York, Philadelphia, Baltimore, Milwaukee, Buffalo, Chicago, Detroit, Lansing, Boston and Cleveland, where there are local food trade unions, there has been co-operation in bringing pressure on food chains and other distributors and retail stores to stop handling California grapes. Boycott activity is also taking place in other American cities, some thirty-five in all.

The initial focus of the boycott was in New York City, which normally receives about one seventh of all the grapes shipped from California. In January 1968, fifty migratory workers traveled three thousand miles in an unheated school bus to the doors of Paul Hall's Seafarers Union, where they received a royal welcome and were given help to take care of their needs. Farm-worker pickets set up lines at Hunt's Point Terminal in the Bronx. They were harassed, threatened and insulted. Early in February 1968, twenty-two pickets were arrested on a charge filed by Hunt's Produce Association. Later the charges were dropped and the boycott continued. In the summer of 1968 the New York City government joined the boycott against California's table grapes. New York has become the hub of prounion and antigrower activity.

One might find the *"Huelga"* banner in other picket lines. When the agents for the Metropolitan Life Insurance Company were on strike, sympathetic farm workers were marching with their banners. One is likely to find someone wearing a button—"Boycott Grapes" or "Viva la Causa"—almost anywhere.

The boycott was almost completely successful in its early stages. Receipts of California grapes in New York between June 10 and July 15, 1968, were virtually zero.

In June California growers filed a complaint with the regional office of the National Labor Relations Board stating that an unlawful secondary boycott had been instituted by the local food trade unions. Under the terms of the agreement, the unions promised not to undertake a specific list of boycott activities and agreed to post a notice on union bulletin boards to that effect.

This opened up the market in New York for some grapes, but the shipments were seriously curtailed. In other cities such as Cleveland, the unions and the chain stores agreed that the stores would continue to stock grapes but each store would prominently display a sign reading: "Please don't buy California table grapes. Help the California grape workers better their living conditions." In Chicago, A&P, National Tea Company, Jewel Tea Company and Hillman's Fine Foods agreed not to purchase California grapes.

The boycott has brought into the picture some of the country's most powerful unions, the AFL-CIO. Walter Reuther marched in the streets of Delano and outside the vineyards in a demonstration of his support for the farm workers. Reuther told a rally of workers that his auto union would contribute "five thousand dollars a month to the cause as long as it would take to win the strike." Seven months later, the AFL-CIO made the strike more than just a token affair; it became a matter of major concern.

Backed by muscle and financing, strikers demanded that markets, school cafeterias, city agencies and buyers and sellers of food quit handling grapes or face picketing. Some large universities have joined the boycott. The University of California at Berkeley has found itself in the midst of the explosive controversy. Up to the end of 1968 there had been campus rallies, one sit-in, eleven arrests and a call for a student strike over the grape boycott. Spokesmen for a Mexican-American student federation said at one point, "We have just begun to get warmed up."

The crisis began when Charles Hitch, president of the university, sent letters to the chancellors of all nine university campuses instructing them that they could stop ordering grapes for the university dining facilities only if there was not sufficient demand for them so as to make continued service uneconomical. He said the university would not take any position on the boycott.

Mr. Hitch's letter was in reply to an action taken in October 1968, by the Berkeley campus purchasing agent's office banning table grapes in the cafeteria and residence-hall dining rooms. The action was taken at the request of the students.

While there are only one hundred Mexican-Americans among Berkeley's 27,000 students, activists involved in other campus protests were backing the boycott. Since students would not eat the grapes and they were rotting on the tables, the university was not buying grapes. Meanwhile, President Hitch came in for criticism from Cesar Chavez in a telegram to the student federation, "Surely the university has a responsibility to do something about poverty, not just study it. Apparently Hitch does not hold that view. These students are demonstrating in a beautiful and nonviolent way that the university should be a servant of the poor and not the tool of the growers."

In Nashville, Tennessee, Scarritt College, Peabody College and Vanderbilt University refused to serve table grapes. Students persuaded grocery merchants to abstain from selling the fruit. In Nashville the officials of A&P at one point had no grapes on hand and none on order. Other chain-store owners were willing to talk to student boycott leaders. Some leaders claimed that the support that the Chavez union received in Nashville had an impact on the South. "The people here in the South are

being used to dump the grapes," said Mrs. Richard
Peterson, a supporter of the boycott, "but we plan to
keep on working until the farm workers' union is recognized."

At Stanford University, students voted to boycott
grapes from their dining halls. Demonstrations have
taken place at Duke University in Durham, North
Carolina.

The most difficult area of the boycott involved the
federal government. The Defense Department during the
boycott continued to buy fresh table grapes for shipment
to Vietnam. As a matter of fact, during the boycott they
stepped up purchases by 40 per cent. One official declared that ". . . this is done only to carry out the
department's duty of meeting the needs of the military
for grapes or anything else." The farm workers charged
that the federal government and some of its agencies
were seeking to subvert the boycott by buying large
quantities for Americans living in Vietnam. A study
made by the United Farm Workers Organizing Committee (AFL-CIO) claimed that since 1965, the year the
union began their strike against the growers, table-grape
exports to South Vietnam rose to an estimated five hundred thousand dollars in 1968. The union study also
showed that Vietnam is the third largest importer of
government-purchased table grapes. The Pentagon said it
had increased its shipment of grapes from 468,000 pounds
in 1967 to 2.5 million pounds in 1969.

Late in 1969 the Farm Workers Organizing Committee
sought a federal injunction to bar efforts that they say the
United States Defense Department is making to break the
grape boycott. The court papers charged that the department "has attempted to raise the price of grapes by
increasing its purchases of grapes from six million nine

hundred thousand pounds in the fiscal year ending in June 1968, to sixteen million pounds in fiscal 1969." The petition stated that the department's increase in purchases violates federal regulations "requiring them to be neutral in labor disputes and to refrain from taking a position on the merits of the labor dispute."

The committee asked that the department be enjoined from increasing its grape purchases above the 1967 level.

According to the June 27, 1969, copy of the New York *Times*, "the Pentagon said it bought 7.5 million pounds of grapes for $1.04-million in 1966, 8.3 million pounds for $1.25-million in 1967, 6.9 million pounds for $1.32-million in 1968 and 11 million pounds for $1.98-million in the fiscal year 1969, which ends June 30."

The Reverend James Drake, a member of the California Migrant Ministry and the national boycott coordinator for the UFWOC said, "These statistics raise the fear that once again the federal government may be acting to break our strike and crush the farm workers' movement. In opening the border to unlimited 'migration' from Mexico during the 1966-67 Texas strike and the 1968 Coachella Valley strike, the Justice Department and the federal government dealt a blow to the efforts to force growers to the bargaining table through traditional strikes and picket-line activity. Now, through government purchasing, the United States may be deliberately seeking to break the consumer boycott of California table grapes, which is proving increasingly effective throughout the country."

The wholesale price of Thompson table grapes, the largest-selling variety, fell from $4.90 to $5.00 a box in July 1968, to $3.00 a box in July 1969, according to the consumer and marketing service of the United States Department of Agriculture. National sales of table grapes dropped from 1243 railroad carlots in the first seven weeks of the 1968 harvest to 1092 railroad carlots in the same period of 1969, according to the Department of Agriculture. A carlot contains about 1500 twenty-four-pound boxes of grapes.

Grapes destined for Southeast Asia moved through San Francisco, where pickets—farm workers, Roman Catholic and Episcopalian priests—blocked grape shipments waiting to be loaded onto ships.

Probably the most dramatic event connected with the boycott took place in Boston, where a "Boston Grape Party" took place. Churchmen joined some one thousand protestors in dumping dozens of crates of grapes into the harbor in a symbolic re-enactment of the famous Boston Tea Party. The demonstrators followed the route of Boston's Freedom Trail to the harbor. The line of march included locals of the Boston Typographical Union, the United Packinghouse Food and Allied Workers Union and the Meat Cutters Union. As they passed down School Street past King's Chapel and the old City Hall, there echoed the hearty chant, "Don't buy grapes."

Mayor White of Boston released an edict prior to the "party" prohibiting city departments from buying grapes.

Once the growers realized that they were not dealing merely with Cesar Chavez, they made their moves. Growers and farm owners led a "givers strike" against those who were involved in the boycott. For example, The Fresno Area Council of Churches suffered financial deficits necessitating the release of staff members, attributed to the "many pressures, economic, social and religious, with many who hold the purse strings disagreeing with the council's stand on the farm labor dispute." The Reverend Herbert W. Neale, the council's president, stressed that the farm labor issue had inflamed tensions within Protestant denominations—conservatives had opposed the support given to the grape pickers, the strike and the boycott.

The growers have had the support of several protest groups. The first group to form was the Mothers Against Chavez, which was made up of farm workers' wives and women farm workers under the leadership of Mrs. Josephine Gabaldon. The women, said Mrs. Gabaldon, were united because they were "fed up with the abuses they and their children were suffering from the organizers." The growers claim that the women have been called obscene names when they refused to quit working. The wives of the men received threatening telephone calls if they did not persuade their husbands to leave their jobs. The farm workers, on the other hand, claimed that Mrs. Gabaldon did not understand the real concerns of the farm worker because she had been a crew boss.

Chief spokesman for the Agricultural Freedom to Work Association has been its general secretary, Jose Mendoza of Bakersfield, California. Since the California Right to Work Committee underwrote his travel expenses, Mr. Mendoza has traveled to various parts of the country to "tell it as it is." In a talk at Atlantic City, New Jersey, he said, "For three years now the United Farm Workers Organizing Committee has failed miserably in its organizing campaign, despite the expenditure of ten million dollars and the nationwide grape boycott." He insisted that beatniks and a handful of union-supported families compose the backbone of the boycott.

State Senator Frank X. McDermott, Republican from Union County, New Jersey, urged the Vegetable Growers Association of New Jersey at the same meeting to develop good management-labor relations with their farm employees in order to thwart becoming targets of the union. He called for fringe benefits, a decent standard-of-living wage and acceptable working conditions. In contrast, Charles M. Creuziger of Sturtevant, Wisconsin, and president of the national vegetable growers group, advocated abolishing the National Labor Relations Board. He labeled it a "labor-oriented kangaroo court."

The farm workers claim that Jose Mendoza is a shoe salesman hired to represent himself as a worker and to spread antiunion propaganda. Said Wayne (Chris) Hartmire of the California Migrant Ministry, "He makes speeches all over the country but has no organization at home, no following among farm workers and is just the most recent example of the willingness of some minority people to sell themselves to the very forces that keep their brothers poor and powerless."

Fighting back against the cross-country speeches of Mendoza has been Vanustiano Olguin, a "brown militant" who is an organizer of grape pickers in California. Mr. Olguin differs from many of the Mexican-Americans that he represents in that he went to college—the University of Redlands. Olguin has been picking grapes since he was six years of age. He went through high school and college through the efforts of his family. He spends a great deal of the "off season" on the road telling the plight of the grape pickers to audiences wherever he finds those willing to listen.

The going for Chavez has not been easy. This is understandable. Allied with the huge landowners are banking interests, such as the Bank of America; the pesticides industry, which includes such giants as Shell Oil Company; the farm machinery manufacturers; Governor Ronald Reagan of California and his administrators, who include such men as Allan Grant, a highly paid professional spokesman for the four-billion-dollar agribusiness industry and a member of the California Farm Bureau Federation; and state chambers of commerce throughout the country. In addition, when Richard Nixon was stumping for the presidency, he publicly ate grapes on his swing through the state.

Along with these individuals are other members of conservative groups. James A. Wechsler, writing in the New York *Post* (March 11, 1969), was critical of William F. Buckley, Jr., and his veteran collaborator, William A. Rusher, for not caring about America's agricultural workers. Said he, "Insofar as this breed of so-called conservatism has any ideological stance with regard to the inhabitants of these lower depths, it might be summarized as the doctrine that migrants shall remain free—regardless of race, color or creed—to labor under the conditions fixed by growers and denied the freedom to achieve recognition for a union of their own choice. As part of the same right wing theology, the struggling grape workers shall be subject to the negative secondary boycott provisions of the Taft-Hartley statute but externally excluded from the positive collective-bargaining protection accorded by law."

The boycott of grapes has produced hassles and has reverberated through staid congressional halls. The congressman from New York told the congressman from California, "I like your grapes but not the sentiment behind them."

The exchange of words and grapes between Representative James Scheuer, D-New York, and Robert Mathias, R-California, took place in the corridor outside the latter's office. The freshman lawmaker from California's San Joaquin Valley, a two-time Olympic decathlon gold medalist, sent bags of muscat and white imperial grapes to all his colleagues. Some were accompanied by bumper stickers that read: "Eat California's grapes—the forbidden fruit."

Scheuer and another New York Democrat personally returned their grapes. Six other House Democrats sent theirs back when they interpreted the move as a slap at the boycott on California grapes.

Police moved in to clear the corridor of the fast-growing crowd of congressional aides, newsmen and a small group of Mexican-Americans who acted as spokesmen for their California co-workers. Just one office down from the scene, Representative Albert Watson, R-South Carolina, lounged in the doorway of his office munching on grapes, with an air of contempt for the protestors.

The boycott has been decisive. It has been costly. It separates many strikers from their families, and it hurts the innocent. It affects both small and large growers. So far, the followers of Cesar Chavez feel that it has been the nonviolent course of action to bring economic pressure on those who can bring an end to the unjust treatment of farm workers and their families.

The boycott has not been without bitterness. But most of this railing has been heaped upon the church, for it is here that the support for Cesar Chavez and his farm workers has come.

CHAPTER 6

A part-time midwife?

THERE is no secret to the fact that in the rich state of California there is a grape strike and boycott. *Presbyterian Life,* a publication of the Presbyterian Church USA, wanted to inform its readers about Cesar Chavez, feeling that the story merited the pages of a denominational magazine because of the deep devotion of Chavez and the religious characteristics of the strike. After the article appeared (October 1,1968) all hell broke loose on the editors of the magazine. Letters flowed in to the editorial offices condemning the article. Over thirty thousand subscribers were lost as angry readers canceled their subscriptions. These former readers did not realize, and could not have cared less, that they were indulging in the same type of boycott that Cesar Chavez was using against table grapes, a boycott they condemned.

From the beginning, Chavez has counted on the concern and the backing of the church. He told me that the church has been a great deal of help to him and his movement. "I think it is a sin for the church to do nothing," he said. "I would rather see the church in total opposition to the poor man than to close its eyes and pretend problems do not exist."

When I asked Chavez what the church specifically could do, he replied, "It could bring the two sides together to negotiate. I desire negotiation—at least just to talk to the growers. The church has the best opportunity to do this.

The church, Catholic, Protestant and Jewish, entered the California grape issue almost at its start. How could it stay out? Its leadership is Catholic, the Mexican-Americans are predominantly Catholic; Chavez counted on the early support of the Catholic Church.

Thanks to the great American spirit of siding with the underdog, churches of all three major faiths and many denominations entered the Delano strike early. Clergy moved into Delano at the beginning of the strike, as they insisted that the farm workers' dispute not only involved labor but also was a moral issue. John Gregory Dunne in an article in *The Saturday Evening Post* (May 6, 1957) wrote, "In its enthusiasm, the Catholic Archdiocese of San Francisco even indulged in a kind of *realpolitik* with strong overtones of blackmail; in a letter to the chairman of Beaulieu Vineyard the archdiocese suggested that since Beaulieu was the major supplier of altar wines to the churches of San Francisco, it behooved it to recognize the NFWA."

How can a person explain the dominance of religion in this movement? Why are the cross and the Star of David familiar symbols when farm workers gather? Why was the image of the Virgin of Guadalupe, the patroness of the Mexican people, carried by the strikers at the head of the line as they marched from Delano to Sacramento? Why are there Masses in fields and on picket lines? Why the nonviolence and fasting and public prayers? How can all this be fitted together with trade unions? How can this be explained in our kind of society where religion seems to be losing its influence outside of a perfunctory prayer at a fund-raising dinner?

The Reverend James Drake, a minister of the United Church of Christ, explained. "Mexicans have a unique understanding of suffering; Mexico is a poor land with a great deal of suffering. Much of the natural suffering has been ritualized, especially in the work of the Franciscans. Mexicans didn't respond much to the missionaries who came with the conquistadors, but when Junípero Serra, the first Franciscan, landed at Acapulco and walked barefoot to Mexico City, this was something they could understand. Mexicans believe that from suffering you get strength rather than death. This expression is made in penitential acts and especially in the Eucharist. When we celebrate the Eucharist in a field or beside a picket line with real grapes and real bread, it has the kind of earthy meaning that it had in the Indian villages before the cathedrals were built. Of the strike, people are saying, 'We've always suffered. Now we can suffer for a purpose.'"

Probably no other group has found more empathy with the farm workers than the California Migrant Ministry. Today there are more migrant ministers in nearly every farming area of the country, carrying on the work started over thirty-five years ago by Lila Bell Acheson Wallace, wife of the publisher of *The Reader's Digest*, and Josephine Gregory Myers. Through its California workers, such as the Reverend Wayne C. Hartmire, Jr., a Presbyterian minister, and the Reverend James Drake, the programs have been directed toward eliminating the underlying causes of poverty and weakness and not merely attempting to eliminate the symptoms. Rather

than operate special "migrant clinics," the California
Migrant Ministry has sought better wages so workers
could buy their own health services for their families.
Mr. Hartmire is the director of the CMM (California
Migrant Ministry), which is supported by the Northern
California Council of Churches and the Council of
Churches in Southern California. Mr. Drake is also associated with CMM and is administrative assistant to
Cesar Chavez and a close associate of the leader. The
relationship of the churches and the farm workers' movement is the story of how one arm of the religious community has penetrated to the heart of an organizing
effort that has an enormous humanizing potential. The
denominations weakly support the CMM but have not
taken its responsibilities seriously. Yet when the crisis
over Delano came, church leadership was drawn through
CMM into the farm labor conflict. As a result, many
churchmen were won to the cause of the farm workers.
Some, such as Father Mark Day, who has often said Mass
in the fields, have devoted their pastorates to the workers.

The California Migrant Ministry received a grant from
the Schwartzhaupt Foundation in 1957, the funds from
which were to be used to provide community-organization training for CMM. This meant going about with
Cesar Chavez or Fred Ross for six to eight weeks as
they concerned themselves with the Community Service
Organization. It also meant working with Saul Alinsky
of the Industrial Areas Foundation.

This training was a beginning commitment on the part
of the staff to the practical business of redistributing
power for the sake of social justice. The traditional forms
of service programs by themselves were seen to be dis-
honest attempts to salve the conscience while hanging on
to an unjust social system which benefits one group of

people, the Anglos, at the expense of the poor. There were risks involved: There would be loss of financial support, loss of rapport with the growers who owned the camps where migrant ministry programs were being carried out, loss of the assistance of church volunteers, local educators and health officials. There were other risks as well, even concerning the personal lives of the staff.

As the migrant ministry became involved with the farm laborers, they began to discuss problems such as the foreign-labor importation under Public Law 78, whereby *braceros* (Mexican citizens brought into the United States temporarily and usually in groups to add to the existing labor force at times of peak activity) entered the country. The staff began to talk to Fred Ross and Cesar Chavez about the need for a farm labor union. Close contacts were formed with the Agricultural Workers Organizing Committee (AWOC), the independent group that merged later with the NFWA to form the present-day United Farm Workers Organizing Committee (UFWOC:AFL-CIO).

As the ministry developed, the denominations were called on to fund specialized ministries in rural fringe communities where migrant workers were settling and year-long ministries were necessary. There were nine projects set up by 1965, ranging from mission churches to neighborhood houses. Each of these involved a minister, a group worker and a community organizer.

From 1961 to 1964 the *bracero* issue erupted into a raging controversy in California because those opposed to the mass importation of labor seemed to be gaining ground. In 1964 Congress refused to extend Public Law 78, mostly because of the role played by the churches. This victory prepared the migrant ministry psychologically for the conflicts that were ahead. Because of the *bracero* issue, the migrant ministry, as was expected, began to lose financial support from the growers and their business associates. For example, J. G. Boswell, who, according to the 1959 Census of Agriculture, owned 32,364 acres of land, and in 1966 received $2,807,633 in soil-bank and acreage-diversion subsidy, cut off $6147 of support in a two-year period. By 1965 a substantial loss had occurred from those people who were willing to support programs that meant hauling food and clothing to migrants but who bitterly opposed social change.

The role of the church in the Delano strike has caused sharp tremors throughout California's Protestant Church community as well as throughout the country. Councils of churches involved in the work began to suffer. The Fresno Area Council of Churches, composed of the major Protestant denominations in the vicinity, had a loss of income partly attributed to the council's support of the strike and boycott against table-grape growers in the San Joaquin Valley. The Reverend Wynn B. Yinger, director of the council, whose position was terminated, charged that the Delano-centered dispute between vineyard owners and grape pickers had led to a growers' strike against the council. He said his dismissal was the culmination of many pressures, economic, social and religious, with those who hold the purse strings and who disagreed with the council's stand on the farm labor dispute.

In an interview he explained his views regarding pressures. Mr. Yinger feared the conservative political and economic action would have grave implications for the future of the San Joaquin Valley, notably depriving it of leadership. "Some believe," he said, "that the church in the valley has not earned the right to speak with authority on such matters as social justice. For instead of being the leader of wholeness and reconciliation, we have too often been that institution which impedes and the one which condones the violence of the *status quo*.

"There are those who would have you believe that there is no significant suffering or need among the majority of farm workers in our valley. I submit that such persons have not been to Arvin, Wasco, Shafter, McFarland, Sanger, Del Rey or East Mendota and all of the miserable farm labor camps hidden away among the coves of plenty."

Fresno County, he continued, is the richest agricultural county in the nation, yet "interns told me that Fresno is a good place for medical study, for we have so much misery among the poor."

Mr. Yinger stated that the boycott was repressive and costly—a kind of court of last resort, but he said that boycott is not new to the church in the valley. "Churches have been exercising it against denominations, councils of churches, the migrant ministry and the newspaper, the Roman Catholic *Central California Register*, for several years. It is more than withholding funds—it means that growers are on strike by refusing to contribute toward positions that involve social change . . .

"The struggle will end someday. What casualties we will find remain to be seen. There will be many, but the continued rigidity, clichés and myths perpetrated by some clergymen can only prolong it. In the end, sadly, the church will have been the least effective servant to farm workers, as well as the small efficient family farmer who suffers grievously in farming today. We have been little more than a part-time midwife to an important birth of justice for all of agriculture."

In 1964 the California Migrant Ministry began an

ambitious project in Tulare County, especially in and around Porterville. The intention was to begin in one area of the county and eventually build a coalition of people's organizations that would change the political characteristics of the county.

The organization's efforts and focus was on the low-income Mexican-Americans, most of whom were seasonal workers. An organization called the Farm Workers Organization (FWO) was developed, limiting its membership to farm workers, so that middle-class Mexicans and Anglos could not join and dominate the organization. Dues were set at two dollars a month. At first there was no intention of becoming involved in labor issues such as wages and working conditions. The FWO worked on such things as the *bracero* issue, voter registration, development of low-income housing, unfair or illegal rents, individual wage claims, welfare issues and such related social areas.

By 1965 the California Migrant Ministry realized that the problem of most concern to the farm worker was his job. His suffering was related to low income and the low regard in which he was held. He cared most about wages and working conditions. Brave Mexican-American leaders began to push the migrant ministry into the areas it least desired at that moment to be in. The migrant ministry staff did not feel competent in the field of labor relations. They were also aware that support from the churches and foundations might be discontinued if the migrant ministry staff became labor organizers.

A close association with Cesar Chavez led to the affiliation of the FWO with Chavez's organization. With this, they gained a credit union, death benefit insurance and relationship to a valley-wide farm workers' group that had collective bargaining as its goal.

In 1965 Cesar Chavez asked the California Migrant Ministry for help in the strike against the growers. The Reverend James Drake and Gilberto Padilla were assigned, with some apprehension, to work with the farm workers. From this point on, there was only one way for the migrant ministry staff to go—to the center of the *bracero* struggle, local community-organization controversies and the drive to organize farm workers into a strong, democratic union.

Said Chris Hartmire, "It is important to note that without this pioneering penetration, the churches would not have been in a position to understand the strikers or support them in their time of need; nor would we have been able to bring our influence and our hopefulness about life to bear in a tense and at times hopeless situation. Gospel communication and influence are tied inextricably to servanthood. There does not seem to be any other way."

On September 20, 1965, the Mexican-American and Filipino workers stayed away from the California grape fields. The strike was on, and the California Migrant Ministry staff was directly involved. A volunteer staff was recruited to assist on the picket line, in the office, with press relations, in developing support and in organizing among members after they left the fields. Clergy were sought out to walk the picket line, assisting the strikers in their nonviolent stance and also reminding the police, grower security guards and growers that the rest of the world was watching. Money was solicited for food to feed the families on strike.

With churchmen leading the way, enough support was enlisted to help the families and keep the strike going. Despite the presence of clergy, some violence erupted on the picket lines and around the town of Delano.

Up to this point, the strike was centered around Delano. The growers regarded the whole issue lightly, insisting that a few agitators were "shooting off their mouths." A clergy visitation team talked with the growers, the workers and public officials; they visited the picket lines and observed the strike at close range. Then they issued a public statement calling on both sides to come to the negotiating table. Nothing happened.

The migrant ministry staff found that police harassment was their most serious problem. Clergy who came into the area were photographed by the police, and the Kern County sheriff admitted he kept a file on all personnel marching in the picket lines.

By October the sheriff's deputies began to limit the activities of the pickets. At first they were told they could not shout to strikebreakers in the fields. Later they were informed they could not even talk to people in the fields. The roving picket lines were trying to cover four hundred square miles of grape vineyards, and in order to persuade workers to join the strike, they had to be able to talk with them.

The jockeying for place and position was not without its humor, despite its seriousness. A young minister from the First Christian Church in Visalia shouted to those workers behind the picket lines a paragraph of Jack London's definition of a strikebreaker. He was immediately arrested. The deputy was so shocked by this passage of literature that he wanted to find the author and arrest him too. On October 19, 1965, forty-four persons, including nine clergymen, went to the picket line determined to communicate with the strikebreakers. They were arrested for shouting *"huelga"* after being warned that they were breaking the law. A Bakersfield judge dismissed the charges on the grounds that they had the constitutional right to stand on public property and read from Jack London. The Kern County attorney dropped the charges against the forty-four. From that point on, the picket lines had the freedom they needed, and soon the strikers were using bullhorns to get their messages to the fields.

The arrests as played up by the press, radio and television brought national attention to Delano. Food and money support increased. Both clergymen and laymen converged on the city every week from all parts of the country.

When the Schenley Industries boycott was announced in December 1965, churchmen went to work to convince the company that many persons would refrain from buying their products unless they dealt justly with their field workers. Churchmen walked the picket line in front of grocery stores and passed out leaflets at retail liquor stores. They continued their activity in the DiGiorgio and Perelli-Minetti boycotts. The march to Sacramento in February and March of 1966 was almost a religious pilgrimage with many hundreds of clergymen and laymen participating. When DiGiorgio announced his own style of union-representation election in June 1966, churchmen visited the workers in Borrego Springs and Delano, talked with them and taped these conversations in order to demonstrate to the governor of California that the election was fraudulent. Eventually the election was dismissed by all parties and another one set up for August 30, 1966. This one was won by Chavez's union and hailed by AFL-CIO president George Meany as the opening of a "new era for farm workers, not only in California but all across the nation."

Churchmen were deeply involved in the DiGiorgio election at their Arvin ranch in October 1966. An interfaith team took part in the Perelli-Minetti Company dispute. Here again many denominations were represented.

The church support was a great help to the strikers at the beginning of the strike. Besides material gifts, they were given essential moral support.

In Cincinnati, Archbishop Clark J. Alter came out strongly on the side of the boycott of California table grapes. He issued a formal statement in which he cited Vatican II documents and called the farm workers "among the forgotten Americans suffering the privation and human indignity of poverty and social injustice." His statement was followed by a message from the Archdiocesan Council of Women which affirmed the UFWOC goal of union representation and federal minimum wages.

The boycott spread to places such as Toronto, Canada. There Sisters Mary Felicia, Mary Francella and Mary Michael of the Felician Order in Port Credit, Ontario, joined one thousand persons at a weekend march to signify the support of the boycott.

One of the larger groups that came out strongly for the boycott was the Interreligious Foundation for Community Organization (IFCO). It asked its twenty member groups to "secure broad citizen support" for the boycott. The IFCO board of directors, which made the appeal, is composed of representatives from national Protestant, Jewish and Catholic church organizations and from local and regional community-development groups.

The National Council of Churches gave a lift to the grape workers on strike on September 13, 1968. Meeting in Houston, Texas, the general board of the council adopted a policy statement approving the general principle of economic boycotts aimed at securing justice. "Farm workers," stated the resolution, "are unfairly singled out in the language of the National Labor Relations

Act for exclusion from the union certification and collective bargaining procedure under the National Labor Relations Board—an exclusion which the National Council of Churches has denounced and sought to eliminate by working for the amendment of the NLRA."

An editorial in the November 25, 1968, issue of *Presbyterian Outlook* contained the following statement: "Fresh grapes do not appear at our home any more. Each of us enjoys eating them, but we have joined the boycott and have refused to buy fresh grapes so that we may, in our small way, help to support Cesar Chavez and the United Farm Workers Organizing Committee.

"There are two sides to every issue. Even Christians will be divided. A Reformed Church publication thinks it not of concern to 'our' people. So it is with the California grape workers' strike; but the time does come when those who profess Christianity must choose sides and be counted . . .

"We all realize the essential service that the farm workers in our country give to all of American society in bringing food to our table, but they have not had an equal share in the prosperity of our nation."

Editorials such as this helped the farm workers to go on despite what seemed at times to be discouraging odds.

There are those such as Ernesto Galarza of San Jose, author of *Merchants of Labor: The Mexican Bracero Story*, who fear that the Mexican-Americans and Negroes, feeling the frustrations of dependence, will line up against the middle-class taxpayers and show the force of the "Brown Power" movement. "The anger it will generate will make the Black Panther movement look trivial," he said.

But Cesar Chavez has struggled to keep his movement

in the spirit of Martin Luther King, Jr.—nonviolent. He believes fervidly in pacific means to his ends. In early 1968 he undertook a twenty-five-day fast, living only on water and Eucharistic wafers. Reading the Bible and the writings of Mahatma Gandhi, he retired to a private retreat in a scruffy Delano gas station owned by the NFWA in order "to recall farm workers to the nonviolent roots of their movement."

When the fast was over, more than six thousand farm workers gathered in Delano's Community Park for a Mass and bread-breaking ceremony. Unable to walk without aid, Chavez, slumped in a chair on a flat-bed truck, took communion beside the late Robert Kennedy. Senator Kennedy addressed the crowd and hailed Chavez as a "heroic figure of our time." At the end, he chanted, "*Viva la causa! Viva* Chavez! *Viva* all of you!"

Too exhausted to speak to the assemblage, Chavez had the Reverend James Drake read a statement following the fast. ". . . Our struggle is not easy. Those who oppose our cause are rich and powerful, and they have many allies in high places. We are poor. Our allies are few. But we have something the rich do not own. We have our own bodies and spirits and the justice of our cause as our weapons."

In the summer of 1968, Chavez was the keynote speaker at the World Plenary Assembly of the International Catholic Movement for Intellectual and Cultural Affairs—commonly called *Pax Romana*—at St. Joseph's College in Philadelphia. The three hundred scholars from forty-six nations gave Chavez a standing ovation. Referring to the assembly's theme, "Four Faces of Poverty," Chavez related the problems among the California farm workers and again emphasized the importance of nonviolence. "Violence is the most perfect way of exploiting the poor, and has been for centuries."

As national attention focused on California after the fast, more church and synagogue groups began to express their support for the farm workers. Rabbi Judea B. Miller and Rabbi Jacob Lantz of Temple Tifereth Israel in Boston made a trip to California to the grape-growing region. They were sent on a fact-finding mission in behalf of both the Massachusetts Board of Rabbis and the New England Terminal Markets Association. They toured the vineyards and spoke to growers and farm workers, to representatives of industry and of the union, including Cesar Chavez.

Their conclusion was that ". . . there definitely is a strike here. Without Federal labor provisions for farm labor, there is little immediate possibility to settle the strike with arbitration or an election. Despite contentions by the growers that the conditions of farm workers in that region are better than those in other regions of the nation, still the conditions that we did find were wretched. We have studied the entire situation and find this to be a moral question. The exploitation and dehumanization of other human beings for the sake of profit is a religious issue.

"The Massachusetts Board of Rabbis has decided, in response to our eyewitness report, to continue its support of the boycott of California table grapes. This is based on the Talmudial principle of *Osek*, the exploitation of the hired man, which is forbidden by Jewish law."

An important exception to a passive or acquiescent role in the Delano struggle has been the action of the board of directors of the United Church of Christ's Board for Homeland Ministries, who on October 31, 1969, released a strong resolution in support of the farm workers:

"The UCBHM reaffirms its support of the goals of the United Farm Workers Organizing Committee and calls upon all churchmen to demonstrate their concurrence by using their purchasing power in behalf of justice. This board reports its action to all churchmen and requests they consider refraining from the purchase of all California table grapes unless it can be positively determined that such grapes have been harvested by union employees."

Are mediation and reconciliation more appropriate roles for the church than such words? Roman Catholic Bishop Timothy Manning of Fresno, the diocese in which Delano is located, mentioned the dispute in a pastoral letter which ordered a Mass in honor of St. Joseph the Worker in every parish in September 1968.

"Before God," Bishop Manning said, "we have tried to give an impartial statement of the teachings of the church on the rights to organize, whether on the part of labor or management. Again and again the bishops of California have urged the intervention of the civil authority for legislation or mediation in this anguished problem.

"To do less, or to remain silent, would be to forfeit the responsibility of teacher, which is inherent in the mission of the church. In fulfilling these duties, there is a strong sharing in the misunderstandings and reprisals that have plagued all labor problems from the beginning.

"In God's name, let us meet at the altar and beg for the charity of reconciliation, remove all bitterness and, as brothers, begin once more to cooperate, to forgive and to understand."

Chris Hartmire said that the workers "want to get together with their employers—not as individuals or in crews, but as an organized body with bargaining power." He feels that reconciliation depends on a balancing of power so that equal communication can take place. The workers must be strong enough to force bargaining. Chris thinks that those who believe in justice and reconciliation should see to it that the workers are on an equal level of bargaining strength with the growers. "This does not mean denying the humanity of employers; it does mean calling on those employers to demonstrate their best humanity by taking their workers seriously at the bargaining table."

Some Christians and Jews have argued that the goals of the farm workers' movement are just, but that the boycott tactic is cruel and unfair. Chavez cannot understand this reasoning, and neither do the members of the migrant ministry staff. In turn, they ask some penetrating questions. What is the alternative? Should the workers merely wait around and hope for things to get better? Is the suffering and denial of the good life to workers and their children more acceptable than the boycott? What about those persons who have justified even killing and destruction for the sake of certain ends, such as in Vietnam to save Southeast Asia from Communism. Wouldn't nonviolence be more reasonable than violence?

Hartmire feels there is a challenge facing the church and church people in the grape issue. "If it is to succeed," he says, "people who care must get off the seat of their pants and do some deeds for justice. Why can't more of us set aside some of our consumerisms and some of our personal and bureaucratic priorities to help concretely that servant community of farm workers that is struggling to break open a new future? Every man's decision about the boycott is important to the shape of the new future."

What is probably the most discouraging aspect of the church and strike situation in California and all over the country is the neutrality of many churches. Despite the willingness of some of the clergy, lay people and church organizations, all too many of our organized churches remain passive. Such a position is considered as an *ipso facto* support of the system now being challenged by the workers. While individuals and individual churches have contributed food, clothing and money, they have skirted the issue, pretended that it does not exist or remained aloof from events in the valley.

The failure of churches to identify with the poor has caused a cleavage between the poor and the church structures. The strike is not without its church friends, but what is lacking is a close relationship to the institutional church. California Presbyterians have reacted in different ways to the strike. Local churches have both supported it and opposed it. The Presbytery of San Francisco has voted to support it. The Presbytery of Los Angeles has defeated a resolution for support and has thus remained neutral. The Episcopal Diocese of San Joaquin has openly criticized the role of the migrant ministry.

The Delano Ministerial Association issued a sharp statement severely criticizing "any ecclesiastical demonstration or interference in the farm labor situation" and reminded the clergy that their concern should be "in the spiritual area."

The local pastors added that "we're here as spiritual leaders to bring people to God. We are not to give advice on economic matters. We resent highly the fact that other clergymen have come into this area and have destroyed the image of the church. There's no moral issue involved. The clergy have no business to be involved."

When Hartmire talked to the pastor of the local Baptist church, a member of the ministerial association, he urged the clergyman to consider at least an effort to talk to the growers about health guarantees in the living areas and fields if he did not want to become involved in economic matters. Came the reply that his "calling to the church was to a higher purpose. Cesar Chavez is not a minister; let him put toilets in the fields."

Chris feels that the church needs to be with the growers as well as with the workers. "Both need the chastisement and the strength of the Gospel as well as the comfort and strength of a message of faithfulness," he says.

But the growers, in answer to the involvement of the church, have rapped the clergy for the support they have given to the strike and the boycott. Allan Grant, president of the powerful sixty-thousand-member California Farm Bureau and president of Governor Reagan's state board of agriculture, has not been hesitant to declare his stand. "The most decisive force in America today," he said, "is the National Council of Churches and its auxiliary body, the California Migrant Ministry."

Mr. Grant, a Presbyterian nonvoting member of the Northern California-Nevada Council of Churches board of directors, claims that the clergy's support of the farm labor movement is a "humanistic horizontal" approach to religion, whereas it ought to be vertical—man's relationship to God. The church, he says, as the body of Christ, is responsible to its Head and must speak with the corporate voice of its members and not its liberal or conservative elements. "The church's role should be redemptive and conciliatory. Are we reconciling man to man when a clergyman with a bullhorn is yelling to the man in the fields and then the clergy asks to be the reconciliatory factor in a dispute? We should be reconciling but not on the picket line."

Louis Lucas, a grower from Delano, also took issue with the church's backing of Cesar Chavez. At a student meeting at Stanford University in which the grape issue was debated, Mr. Lucas and John Bree, both officers of the South Central Farmers Committee, which represents the growers, lashed out at the clergy for "adding dignity to a cause that is without dignity."

In answer to those who desire that the church not be involved in conflict, Dr. John C. Bennett, president of Union Theological Seminary in New York, feels that "churches have responsibility to help in the development of forms of power among the powerless in order to counteract the persuasive power of the strong . . . It is a great advance when people who have been powerless, who have been governed chiefly by apathy or fatalism, organize to improve their lot, and this means creating instruments of political and economic power that enable their interests to be felt by the community at large . . . The local church in a neighborhood of deprivation and injustice should not hold aloof from this struggle."

At the same time, Dr. Bennett feels that the church must remain the "mother of us all." While it includes the poor and the rich, those in the city, the town and the suburb, it must seek to heal and change—to be all inclusive and at the same time to stand for something.

What will happen if farm workers do not get more support than pious declarations and preaching from men of good will? Fresno Mayor Floyd Hyde is worried. "We have left the poor people of the San Joaquin Valley no alternative, and there are growing signs that they realize it. We are pushing them toward violence."

The die was cast. In Texas, Ed Krueger watched the California developments. As the church in California was drawn into the farm labor issue there, it was also drawn into the problems of the Rio Grande Valley. The role it was to play among Mexican-Americans has to a large extent shaped the direction the church of the future would take regarding the pressing problems that face our country today.

Only the church's active involvement can prevent a confrontation with "Brown Power."

CHAPTER 7

Violence involves Krueger in the Rio Grande Valley

ED KRUEGER was well aware of what was taking place in California—new concepts of thinking among Mexican-Americans, the leadership of men like Chris Hartmire, Jim Drake and Cesar Chavez, the idea of a union among farm workers and the involvement of the church. The whole panorama of the plight of the Mexican-Americans was an interplay that stretched from valley to valley, from San Joaquin to the Rio Grande.

As events continued to unfold in south Texas, the powerful influence of events in the Far West had a strong bearing on Ed Krueger. Things were big in California, headline catching. Millions of dollars were involved along with thousands of people and the economy of one aspect of the land. But Cesar Chavez had not forgotten his people in Texas. And Ed Krueger unwittingly became entangled in the maze.

The crowds participating in *La Marcha* of 1966 left Austin and returned to the long, slow, difficult task of building the union and organizing fellow workers. Many of the farm workers had migrated north to Colorado, Wisconsin and Michigan and first heard of the union activities when they returned. In cafes, in bars, in door-to-door canvassing, the message of the cause was taken to every *barrio* and hamlet along the valley. County political machines swung into action, as they feared any change in the *status quo*. Efforts and plans began to take form to break the strike and frighten the people. The growers looked to Mexico to supply workers for the late fall crops and for winter work.

We have seen how Gene Nelson, a strike captain in Delano, had aroused the hopes of the Mexican-American workers in the Rio Grande Valley. Stumping through the small towns, he assured the workers that a share of the better life was to be had if they would organize into a union. Gene felt that the time was ripe, so he signed up seven hundred workers for his newly formed union—the Independent Workers Association (IWA).

MAJOR AGRICULTURAL MIGRANT DEMAND AREAS

WINTER

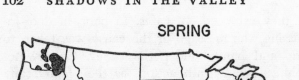

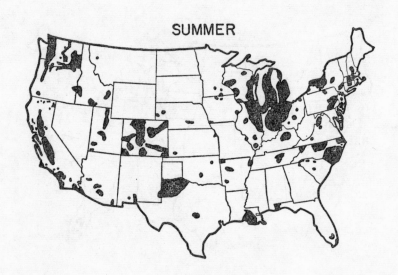

FALL

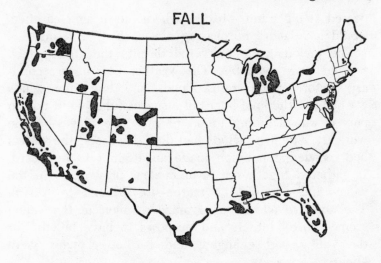

Feeling strong enough for action, on June 1, 1966, the union called a strike, well after the melon-picking season got under way in the valley, against three of the larger melon farms and five packing sheds where the melons were brought from the farms, sorted, stamped, crated and loaded into refrigerator cars. The workers asked for $1.25 an hour and a contract between the IWA and the growers. Within twenty-four hours a temporary restraining order had been obtained by the growers which prohibited pickets at the struck farms.

Despite the court order, the strike was kept alive by rallies and marches in the valley communities. The growers, concerned that millions of dollars in melons would rot in the fields, sent trucks and word to Mexican border towns that green-card workers would be welcome. And the strikebreakers came! Wetbacks, also hearing that work was available, came across the Texas border, collected their wages at the end of the day and disappeared at night into Mexico, where the meager earnings would have more purchasing power than in Texas.

The melons were marketed despite the strike, since workers were available. The weather became a secondary factor. Heavy rains, floods and hurricane winds washed out the final hopes of a successful attempt on the part of the fledgling union to raise the wages of the workers. When the winds had died down and the waters had receded, the union made an attempt to be heard. It gathered together a loyal nucleus of workers in the valley and organized a march—*La Marcha*—to Austin. The abortive efforts to organize a union in the valley seemed to all intents and purposes to have failed. But the valley had changed, and further changes were about to appear.

In order to focus public attention on the problem concerning the green-card workers, members of the United Farm Workers Organizing Committee placed a picket line on the international bridge at Roma on October 24, 1966. Cars of the green carders working on the struck farms were persuaded to turn back to Mexico. Other cars were allowed to go though. Eugene Nelson was arrested by sheriff's deputies, resulting in more confusion and delays. The pickets sat down on the bridge in protest of Nelson's arrest and thus blocked all traffic between the United States and Mexico. Deputy Sheriff Adolfo Ramirez and his men dragged off and arrested thirteen persons. Three of them—Gene Nelson, Bill Chandler and Tony Orendain—were found guilty of obstructing a public bridge, a traffic violation, and were fined twenty-five dollars each. Charges against a sixteen-year-old-minor, Guillermo de la Cruz, were not pressed, and the remaining nine adults were exonerated by the judge.

On November 16, 1966, a report issued by a Starr County grand jury called the farm workers' strike "unlawful and unAmerican" and "abusive of rights and freedom granted them as citizens." The grand jury report continued, "The means as are practiced by the union group in Starr County are directly contrary to everything we know in our American and lawful way of life." The report called for the President of the United States to send men into the area "to assist in preserving the rights of all concerned" and for representatives of the Attorney General's office and a Texas Ranger to remain in the county to assist local officers "during these extraordinary times." The report complained of violence and threats by farm workers.

Mr. Morris Atlas, the brilliant and able attorney for La Casita Farms, Inc. and a member of the board of directors of the company and a stockholder, was quoted in *Concern* as saying, "Several workers threatened to kill people and burn the courthouse down. I'm not saying they would have. I'm not saying that if a person says he is going to shoot himself, he is going to do it, but I get alarmed just because he says it."

The year 1967 was full of hope and promise; a new year and a new melon season were approaching. Union members had learned to "sell" their program to the farm workers and migrants. The growers of Rio Grande City and Starr County officials in a fear of violence retaliated by deputizing over forty new sheriff's deputies, including the assistant manager of La Casita Farms. The situation became tense. Arrests began to be made. Two arrests were made on the Starr County Courthouse steps when union leaders, including Gilbert (Gil) Padilla, were charged with "disturbing the jailer" on the third floor as they were saying the Lord's Prayer. In January

five priests and five workers were arrested for trespassing and using "abusive language"; they were shouting,
"*Viva la huelga*." On January 26 ten pickets were arrested
and another ten on February 2. Union members, organizers and strike leaders seemed to be singled out for
arrest as May and the big melon harvest approached.

In January 1967, Jesus Salas, head of the Wisconsin
farm labor union, Obreros Unidos, spent two weeks in
his home town of Crystal City, Texas, where the population is 70 to 80 per cent Mexican-American. He particularly noted changes in the valley since the abolition of
the poll tax. "Now," he observed, "political organizations
are developing the Mexican-American *barrios* or neighborhoods." Salas felt that part of the farm labor problem
must be political.

As to the Texas struggle, he said, "The strike doesn't
put economic pressure on the company, because the
green carders are available and because there is a law
against mass picketing which says demonstrators must
be separated by a distance of fifty feet. The farms are
huge, and a picket may not have much effect because it
passes nearly unobserved . . . I never saw more Texas
Rangers in one area in my life than there are in Roma."

At Easter 1967, the church publicly entered the picture in the Rio Grande Valley. The Catholic bishops of
Texas released a statement calling on farm workers to
organize: "We, the Catholic bishops of Texas, would re-
mind farm workers that among the basic rights of a human person is the right of freely founding associations
or unions for working people . . . Included is the right
of taking part in the activities of these unions without
risk of reprisal. In view of the present depressed state of
farm workers . . . we say that they have a duty to form
and join unions or associations . . ." Added to the state-

ment was a plea for the extension of the National Labor Relations Act to cover farm workers.

The same Easter weekend some 250 college students, including teachers, formed a "Caravan for Justice," by which they retraced the four hundred miles the marchers had taken to the capital the previous year. Fifty-three cars were loaded with two tons of food and medicine for the strikers, together with $2300 raised for the strike effort.

On May 11, 1967, the Confederation of Mexican Workers (CTM) put up a picket line on the Mexican side of the Roma and Camargo international bridges to the United States. On the American side, seventy pickets marched back and forth. The melon harvest, described as the best in five years, had now begun.

On the first day of the picketing, not a single green carder crossed the bridge. Workers on both sides of the bridges formed close friendships and demonstrated a feeling of solidarity. Mexicans are forbidden by law to cross a picket line where the red and black flag of CTM is displayed. "But," said a union official, "politics got involved, especially in Mexico, so the pickets were withdrawn on the Mexican side after two days. Green-card Mexican nationals, driven by hunger and poverty in their own country, began again to cross the river, and American workers became less willing to leave the fields since they knew that there were unlimited numbers of Mexicans to break the strike and take their jobs."

Gil Padilla, vice-president of the UFWOC, who had been sent from California by Cesar Chavez to the Rio Grande Valley to take charge of the operations, tried to keep the picketing going on a twenty-four hour basis but was unsuccessful.

In Austin, state AFL-CIO leader, Ray Evans, charged

before Governor John Connally that the Texas Rangers had taken sides against the farm pickets. An official of the Texas Department of Public Safety replied that "the Rangers are there just to see that the laws are enforced."

A newspaper report alleged that Texas Ranger Captain Alfred Y. Allee was lecturing the pickets, telling them there would be no money for anyone if the melons rotted in the fields. Said Evans, "We do not think this is fair for a law officer to take sides. During the strike on both sides of the bridge, Rangers and Starr County officers watched the Miguel Aleman demonstrations from the Texas side as they talked with management officials from La Casita Farms."

Union officials were bent on maintaining a stance of nonviolence in the Texas Valley as Chavez was determined on doing in California. Explaining the union's position, David Lopez, a former newspaperman with experience in Laredo, Corpus Christi and Austin, who described himself as an "inside agitator" and who had worked for several years on the national staff of the AFL-CIO, said that the union would reject any member caught perpetrating violent acts against growers and their property. "We have been very careful to avoid any evidence and to avoid any unwelcome acts," Lopez said. "Yet here we have not only an unusually large contingent of local peace officers who, in fact, outnumber our pickets but also a dozen or so Texas Rangers, known for their violence, coming into the city."

By the time the melon season had arrived in the Rio Grande Valley, the church had become truly involved. Not only was this evident in the march to Austin and through individual announcements as well as those of the Roman Catholic bishops, but it also could be seen through the establishment of the Valley Team Ministry of the Texas Council of Churches (TCC). In March the TCC had authorized the establishment of a two-man ministry in the valley to serve the workers and the growers. The ministry to the former was to consist of counsel, assistance to families in need and a presence among the Mexican-Americans. It did not include joining in the picket lines or taking part as an organizer. The minister to the grower was to be an expert in agricultural marketing and an aid to farm groups seeking to establish better marketing facilities.

The first team member, the Reverend Edgar A. Krueger, was found and hired in March 1967. Although an honest effort was made, the second member of the team was not found. It was not long before Ed became a controversial figure in the valley. He was seen among the demonstrators and was described by the particularly biased valley press, television and radio as a union organizer, and at the very least, a strike supporter. "All I was doing," Ed told me, "was telling the demonstrators to keep their activities nonviolent and to obey the law that required picketers to remain fifty feet apart."

On May 26, 1967, Ed was on his way to Rio Grande City to give the invocation at a Friday union meeting. He was called to do this by the striking farm laborers, occasionally at first, then more frequently. When he arrived at Rio Grande City, he discovered, much to his chagrin and consternation, that he had not been properly informed; there was no meeting in Rio Grande City, Instead, the union members were in the lower valley at Mission, Texas. So Ed turned his 1959 Rambler around and headed back to Mission. He suspected that something was in the wind; he had heard that the striking workers were going to try to stop a train loaded with melons from the struck farms. Ed was in a hurry. "I felt that I had to persuade them not to carry out their threat, because the union had run out of bail money."

When he arrived at the railroad depot in Mission, he met his wife. As he talked to the strikers, he was arrested by Ranger Captain A. Y. Allee for allegedly creating a disturbance by standing on the tracks in a manner designed to prevent the passage of the train.

When Ed's wife tried to get a picture of his arrest, she too was arrested. Mrs. Krueger claimed in her testimony in the United States District Court meeting in Brownsville (June 11, 1968) that Ranger Allee grabbed her husband by the neck and the seat of his pants and hustled him into the Ranger car. She also said that a Ranger grabbed her after she tried to run away from him and took her camera and exposed some film she had taken of the arrest of the union men.

"Then," she continued, "a Ranger slapped my husband in the car and told him, 'You're not a preacher. If you were, you'd stop these people. You're nothing but a troublemaker.'" Ed testified that a Ranger slammed him against the hood of a car, slapped him and forcibly shoved him into a patrol car.

One reporter wrote that an arresting Ranger said, "Krueger, I'm tired of seeing you around here."

Ed and his wife were driven to Edinburg "at high speeds" to the jail, where they and fourteen others who were arrested were charged with unlawful assembly. They spent twenty hours in jail and were released on five-hundred-dollar cash bond each, a figure two and a half times the maximum fine provided by law for the offense with which they were charged. Following this incident, the Texas Council of Churches decided to file a petition on behalf of the Kruegers, a student arrested with them, Alejandro Moreno, Jr., and Manuel L. Becerra, Jr., a teacher, for an injunction against the Texas Rangers and A. Y. Allee, Tyler Dawson, Jack Van Cleve, Frank G. Horger, and Deputy Sheriffs of Starr County Rene A. Solis, Roberto Pena and Raul Pena.

The complaint of the Texas Council of Churches was filed in the United States District Court for the Southern District Court of Texas in Brownsville. The council did not petition for the punishment of the Rangers but through their attorneys—Hill, King and McKeithan of Mission, Texas—asked only that they be enjoined "from any means, including orders, threats, arrests, confinement, or physical assault, preventing plaintiffs or the members of their class or other representatives of the Texas Council of Churches from going peacefully and lawfully to any public place or private place where they are invitees or licensees, or preventing them from photographing any occurrence connected with the labor unrest; or preventing them from peacefully and lawfully assembling and exercising fully and freely their rights of free speech and of liberty, providing that nothing in said injunction be construed to affect, prevent, prohibit or interfere with the defendants and their deputies, agents, servants, and employees from the lawful discharge of the duties of their offices."

The Catholic bishops of Texas, acting through the Texas Catholic Conference of which they are the board of directors, on July 3, 1967, issued a statement congratulating the Texas Council of Churches for instituting the suit in the federal court at Brownsville protesting the conduct of the Texas Rangers in the Rio Grande Valley and insuring the rights of Krueger and others.

The text of the statement said: "Recently there have been reports in the press of the abuses of persons by

Texas Rangers in Starr County and elsewhere in that area of Texas. If these reports are true, in whole or in part, it is a shameful disgrace to the entire state of Texas and appropriate remedial action is called for. In addition to the serious question, inherent in the reported accounts, regarding the possible use of the police forces of the state to unduly interfere with the churches carrying out a legitimate ministry . . . Not only do we congratulate the Texas Council of Churches for its action, but we appreciate the fact that by bringing this suit it is helping to insure the preservation of the rights of all persons and all churches, and this regardless of the outcome of the suit."

The statement of the bishops concluded that a full-scale trial and public disclosure of the facts "is essential in the public interest . . . we applaud its (TCC) members and its leaders and sympathize with them in the difficult situation into which they have been thrust."

Probably the most thoroughly publicized of the Ranger-union struggles involved the arrest of striking workers Magdaleno Dimas and Benjamin (Benito) Rodriguez on the evening of June 1, 1967.

Here is Dimas's account of the incident as he recalled it in a taped interview for a fact-finding Consultation for Farm Labor Relations in the Lower Rio Grande Valley held in Corpus Christi:

"Me and Beni [Benito Rodriguez], we're fix'n to kill some rabbits, you know, go to the ranch for a couple hours to hunt some rabbits. Somebody gave us a ride. We walk over there to the woods looking for some rabbits, you know. We didn't find no rabbits; a chachalaca bird is what I killed, that's all. We fix'n to go home, cook that chachalaca and eat that chachalaca. Then we walk along the highway. Some guy—I don't know his name—

came along, give us a ride. 'Which way you want to go? You want to go to your home, or where you want to go?' he say. I say I want to go to Beni's house because we're fix'n to cook that chachalaca and eat him over there. I give the chachalaca to Kathy, Kathy Baker, and tell her to go ahead and cook chachalaca for us, you know. Kathy cook for us, and after she cook for us she stay and eat with us. We stayed over there and talked and listened to the radio, probably about an hour when Bill Chandler come by the house and said, 'Hey, Dimas, the Texas Rangers looking for you.' And I tell him, 'What did the Texas Rangers want?' He say, 'I don't know. What did you do?' I say, 'I didn't do nothing. I do nothing. Why?' 'Well, looks like something wrong to me because he was looking for you. Better be careful,' he say, 'because there's going to be hell to pay if he catches you.'

'We're fix'n to go over to my house, you know, when Bill and Arino walk in front and I walked out with my .22, fix'n to go on home. I got over close to the car —I see one car, you know, when they put the lights on— Bill say, 'He's a Texas Ranger! Put the gun down.' And I put the gun down, you know, when I see the Texas Ranger with a shotgun in his hand, and I thought he was sure gonna shoot me or something. I went in the house, and I was standing at the table in the dining room for nine or ten minutes when I heard somebody break one window. I don't know if it was the local people, you know, the cops, the sheriff, local deputy sheriff or the Texas Ranger, I don't know who break that window. And after that, somebody kick the door open. Captain Allee, I guess he was the one that kicked the door. And they break the door and started to break the other one, but the other one was not locked. They hit the door and, you know, it open real easy. And he say, 'Put your hands down, you son-of-a-bitch. You play rough, I'll play rough.' (Bill say that Captain Allee told the other Ranger to 'kill that son-of-a-bitch.' He was outside, you know.)

"Anyway, when they say about four or five times, 'Put your hands down,' I figured out if I put my hands down they gonna shoot me or something, and I just keep my hands up. And then Beni walk close-like to the cops, you know. When he pass Captain Allee, Captain Allee hit him with gun on his neck, put him down. And I thought Beni was already dead because they hit him real rough like you were going to kill a hog or something.

"When I was walk by, Captain Allee hit me on my head. They put me down. I remember passing out, you know, and the other Texas Ranger, they hit me again. They put me down. When I got up Captain Allee hit me over here on my neck. I remember the hit on the neck. I know nothing. I just went down. I felt like it was swimming or somethin', you know. Seemed real dark. And I remember also when I was out somebody hold me from one arm and the other arm and he say, 'Lean down, come on down, and I was coming down like a bird when everybody come and kick me, started kicking me everywhere. And I guess I passed out again, I don't know. I didn't see nothing, you know. I remember I was walking over there and they held my arms again. I remember I was walking out of the house and was standing close to the car when Robert Pena come and hit me with his shotgun with the barrel on my back."

According to some press releases and a report by the Corpus Christi consultation, Dr. Ramiro Casso, who treated Dimas in McAllen, diagnosed him as having a brain concussion and bruises about the face and body. Rodriguez was reported to have had a fingernail torn off as well as having bruises over his body. Dimas,

after first aid, was admitted to a hospital where he was
certified by physicians retained both by the union and the
growers to have been severely beaten, with possible con-
cussions. The arresting charge against Dimas was "disturbing the peace" and "rudely displaying a deadly
weapon."

Magdaleno Dimas was particularly vulnerable from a
legal point of view. He had a long record of arrest and
conviction. At the time of his arrest by the Rangers,
he was a federal parolee. He had been convicted on a
murder charge and served five years for that offense. So
when a group such as the UFWOC were engaged in
social reform and conflict, people "on the other side"
were quick to point a finger and cry that criminal elements form the ranks of the union.

Yet David Lopez does not castigate Dimas. "He has a
police record, a black police record," says Lopez. "But
since he joined the union he has not had so much as a
drunk and disorderly charge, and in our opinion, he has
developed tremendously. We feel this is very symbolic
of what is happening here. People who are in despair
and have no hope of breaking out of the substandard
living rut certainly would tend to drink and misbehave.
But once you give them an opportunity to do something
for themselves, a sense of worthiness is created that
carries them over whatever wrongdoing they have committed in the past."

Ed Krueger also defended Dimas. "I saw Magdaleno
in action on the Friday before his arrest, and I would
not hesitate to say anywhere that I am very proud of
the way he was able to handle himself, of his nonviolent
posture. I saw him taken into the center of the street
from where he had been sitting. He was eating a hamburger at the time. The hamburger was slapped out of

his hand by one of the Rangers, and then one of them proceeded to hit him with a tremendous force in the face. In spite of this deliberate provocation, in spite of the hostility exhibited toward him when he had not been doing anything wrong, Magdaleno did not resist arrest, did not utter a curse, did not say anything back to the Rangers, did not retaliate with any sort of violence. After slapping him in the face, the Ranger proceeded to hold him just a few inches from a passing railroad train, pushed him toward the Ranger car and slammed him forcibly against the car and later shoved him into the car. In all of this, I saw no violence exhibited at all on the part of Magdaleno. His whole attitude was one of accepting the hostility shown toward him."

Trial dates for those arrested in the valley were not set—they were, as a matter of fact, hard to come by. However, as we shall see in our next chapter, the courts became the scene of charges and countercharges.

CHAPTER 8

Rangers deny brutality

FROM early childhood, the Texas Rangers have had a kind of "heroic" image in my mind. Perhaps it was because when as a youngster I went to see Westerns in the old movie houses, the Rangers were portrayed as preserving law and order. They were the ones who rode up majestically on their horses, shot the "bad guys" with perfect accuracy and rescued people in distress. Now that the television stations are showing the old Westerns on the late shows, or as it seems, around the clock, and have featured the Rangers in a series of their own, our children have also had an admiration for the Rangers. The folklore about the Texas Rangers is colorful and extensive, and although in 1968 they numbered but sixty-two, they still carry a special aura. But there are chinks in their shining armor.

When I was in Texas in February 1969, Ed Krueger and I stopped in a small Texas community where by sheer accident we met a Mexican-American old-timer who, because of his age, had become blind. But his mind was still keen and active. We sat on the enclosed screened porch with his aged wife and two sons as he talked with us. His family requested that I not take any pictures. What the old man said about the Rangers kept us spellbound—his recollections were not exactly what I remembered seeing on television.

"I remember," he said, "the time many years ago when the Rangers came to our village and said, 'We are going to burn it down. Move out!' So we gathered a few of our belongings, and sure enough, the next day the whole village was burned to the ground.

"One of the Rangers had a good friend in a house on the edge of town. Several nights after the village burned, under cover of darkness the Ranger slipped over to his friend's house, knocked on the door and urged him to step out into the shadows.

"'What do you want, Ed?' asked Juan, puzzled because of the secrecy.

"'Listen, you life is in danger. Get out of this area. Go someplace, but don't stay here!'

"'But why? I haven't done anything. Why should I leave my home? It's not much, but it's all I've got. I have nowhere else to go.'"

The old man faced us, leaning forward and speaking quietly. "The next day Juan was picked up by the Rangers. He disappeared; no one knows where. His family or his friends never heard from him again."

This is a part of Ranger history that is not often told by those who can still remember, and yet it needs to be told. Many Mexican-Americans do not have a high regard for the Rangers, who are not only the lowest-paid law-enforcement unit in Texas but also have a somewhat dubious present-day reputation. Perhaps it is only legend, but it is said in the valley that the Texas Rangers used to ride their horses and use Mexicans for target practice.

"They'd see a Mexican in the field and just shoot at him. They've had that attitude from the beginning. Now things are a little more civilized, a little more modern. But I don't think much of the Rangers. They've been idealized and they have been praised, but they are not really like that." So spoke an educated and enlightened Mexican-American in Rio Grande City.

Therefore, when the injunction trial between the Texas Council of Churches and the Rangers and Starr County deputies began in the old Starr County Courthouse, it was not surprising that the scenario reminded one of an old movie script. Doug Adair, who edits the Texas edition of *El Malcriado,* the voice of the farm workers, describes it:

"A detachment of Rangers sat in the jury box watching the proceedings. Dressed in their fancy cowboy boots, their badges freshly shined, their big hats in their laps, most of them smoking big cigars, and their six-shooters at their sides, they added to the nineteenth-century feeling that pervaded the courtroom. As each Ranger testified he would ceremoniously unfasten his holster and cartridge belt and leave it on his seat before taking the oath. Captain Allee, his cigar clenched between his teeth, assured his friend the judge that he had never pushed, hit, kicked or beaten anyone unnecessarily.

"The old fans drifted lazily around from the ceiling, sometimes muttering and sometimes coughing and sometimes silent but never having any perceptible effect on the 100-plus heat. The paint peeling off the walls led one to forget that this is a rich county, with a big oil and cattle industry and a six-million-dollar melon harvest in addition to its peppers, cabbages, carrots and other crops. Only the workers—and the government—are poor. It seems that the county could not afford a clock for the courtroom, so Coca-Cola had provided one, with appropriate advertising. During some long-forgotten trial, the clock had stopped at 8:52 and never moved since. The room, the Rangers, the judge, all seemed so unreal, an anachronism in the twentieth-century. But they are real and a very harsh reality for the workers who are trying to build a union in the face of their opposition. All union members know that the county jail cells are upstairs, directly above this very same courtroom."

In June 1968, one year after the suits were filed, the action shifted from the old courthouse to Brownsville, Texas, to the federal court. A three-judge court—U. S. 5th Circuit Court of Appeals Judge John R. Brown of Houston and U. S. District Judges Woodrow Seals also of Houston and Reynaldo Garza of Brownsville—was impaneled because the UFWOC, AFL-CIO, not only filed suit on conspiracy allegations contending that public law-enforcement officers were trying to break up the union but also challenged the constitutionality of six state statutes. Defendants from Starr County were Sheriff Rene A. Solis, Sheriff's Deputies Raul Pena and Roberto Pena, Special Deputy Jim Rochester and Justice of the Peace B. S. Lopez. Plaintiffs were Francisco "Pancho" Medrano of the United Auto Workers, Kathy Baker, David Lopez, Gilbert Padilla, Magdaleno Dimas and Benjamin Rodriguez.

The highlight of the trial was the testimony of Texas Ranger Captain A. Y. Allee, who told the court during his two-and-a-half-hour attestation that he did not care whether the farm workers' union won or lost the strike against the large-scale farms in Starr County.

"They can strike from now until doomsday," said the Ranger captain. "I don't care as long as it is done peacefully." Declaring that he had no interest in the farm labor dispute, he insisted, "I'm not prejudiced." Yet in his original complaint against the Rangers, David Lopez, the union organizer, had said that "We had no reason to fear them, but because the first thing they did upon arrival in Starr County was to spend three hours in consultation with Ray Rochester at La Casita Farms, we requested they pay a similar visit to us. I personally went up to Ranger Jack Van Cleve . . . he pushed me back six feet. Not once have the Rangers visited our headquarters."

Captain Allee, a Ranger since 1931, heads Company D detachment, which patrols thirty-six counties in south Texas with a large Mexican-American population. The captain is a big bluff man who likes to smoke cigars. Asked whether he conferred with the growers, he said he had known some of the ranchers "for a good while" because he had been "in and out of Starr County for thirty-two years." But he stressed that the growers did not talk to him about the strike situation.

At the testimony, Captain Allee also denied that on May 26, 1967, in Mission he had held Ed Krueger inches from a passing train loaded with melons. Questioned by union attorney Chris Dixie of Houston regarding his holding the minister's face near the train, Captain Allee remarked, "That's the biggest falsehood that's ever been made. I never held any face or anybody close to that train."

However, shortly before the trial was adjourned, Dixie produced a head-on photograph showing partially obscured Rangers holding Mr. Krueger and union member Magdaleno Dimas close to the tracks. The photo taken for the Associated Press was allegedly snapped the "instant" the last freight car had passed them.

By a process of elimination, Dixie reasoned that the

Ranger holding the minister was Captain Allee. As several Rangers crowded near the judge's bench to examine the photo, the captain said, "Let it go as me, Judge. I don't care."

Moments later, Ranger Jack Van Cleve said he was the officer pictured with Reverend Krueger. The other Rangers agreed.

The six statutes challenged by the union included laws concerning mass picketing, secondary boycotting, disturbing the peace, unlawful assembly, use of abusive language and obstructing a public road.

The union attorney during the trial attempted to show that the statutes are not only unconstitutional, because the laws are so sweeping they can be enforced selectively or on the basis of discrimination, but also that the defendants applied the laws in such a way as to harass the strike effort to prevent the union members and their sympathizers from exercising their rights guaranteed by the First Amendment to the U. S. Constitution. Dixie also alleged several picketers were told in the Starr County Courthouse by sheriff's deputies, "Never say that again in the courthouse," and a cocked pistol was pointed at them when they shouted, *"Viva la huelga."*

At the conclusion of the one day's proceedings before the three-judge court, Hawthorne Phillips of the Texas attorney general's office, representing the Rangers, Starr County officials and laymen, renewed a motion that the union's suit be dismissed.

The defense attorneys contended that each of the six challenged state laws was valid. Attorney Luther Jones, a spokesman for the defense, told the *Alamo Messenger,* a Catholic newspaper published in San Antonio, also reported in the San Antonio *Express* (June 12, 1968) by the Associated Press, that if the union had any com-

plaints against the defendants involved, it should seek
redress for the grievances in state courts or before a lone
federal judge and then go through normal channels of
appeal.

After the union rested its case the morning of June
12, 1968, Attorney Phillips called Starr County officials,
law-enforcement officers and Texas Rangers to the stand.
They all testified that they were trying to enforce the
law impartially and that they had not entered any agreement with the struck farms to crush the strike.

Defense witnesses testified that the union harassed
four workers at the large farms by taunting them with
obscenities during the picketing activities or by intimi-
dating field hands in an effort to make them stay away
from their jobs. Defense attorneys disclosed that two of
the union members—Magdaleno Dimas and Benjamin
Rodriguez—had criminal records. By the time of the trial,
both men were disassociated from the UFWOC.

Dimas allegedly told La Casita foreman and Special
Deputy Jim Rochester, "I'm going to get you." Rochester
testified that he considered the statement a threat. A
deposition by Captain Allee stated that Jim Rochester
had complained that Dimas appeared near the La
Casita Farms in a pickup truck carrying a rifle. Rochester
testified that he fired two shots at the parked truck and
at the "car" as the men drove away. Dimas and Rodriguez, as we have read, were arrested for displaying the
gun. Although both men claimed they were severely
beaten the night they were arrested, Captain Allee testified that he had used reasonable force in apprehending
the two in the house of Kathy Baker, rented by the
union in Rio Grande City.

"I just cracked him slightly on the head one time with
a shotgun barrel," the Ranger captain was reported to

have said. Captain Allee said he didn't know what caused the bruises but added that as Dimas and Rodriguez left the room where they were arrested, they fell over each other.

Captain Allee also had some harsh words for the Reverend Krueger. He said he had witnessed the minister participating in the union's daily picketing activities. "That preacher," Captain Allee said, "was ramrodding the whole thing." The union members, he added, seemed to follow the Reverend Krueger more than Domingo Arrendondo, head of the UFWOC local in Rio Grande City. Acknowledging the Reverend Krueger as a "preacher," Captain Allee said, "I never saw him preaching."

The Ranger said that during the arrests of several union members at Trophy Farms on May 18, 1967, Ed Krueger had asked him why he didn't also place the clergyman in jail "with my people." "I told him I wanted to treat him with respect," the captain said.

However, during the incident in Mission, Captain Allee said, the United Church of Christ minister had renewed his plea to be arrested after some union members had been apprehended on the railroad right of way, which is located on the community's main street. "Krueger asked me again to put him in jail," the captain testified. "I told him, 'This is the second time you've told me to do this, and I'm sure going to accommodate you.'"

Captain Allee said that after he arrested Krueger, Dimas, who was eating a hamburger, approached him and began talking excitedly. "He was spitting mustard in my face, so I slapped the hamburger out of his hand." He told Attorney Dixie, "I think you would have done the same thing."

Captain Allee said he grabbed Ed Krueger by his

belt, took him toward the railroad tracks and turned him over to another Ranger, who waited for the trains to pass. After the trains had passed, it was noted, the Ranger crossed the tracks and took the minister to the car. Ranger Van Cleve later testified that Ed Krueger and Dimas were held some five or six feet from the tracks.

Not everyone thought that Captain Allee was mistreating Ed Krueger. In a letter to the editor of *Valley Evening Monitor* in McAllen, Clark Atteberry of Mercedes commented on the arrest of Ed Krueger and the grabbing of him by the belt and the seat of the pants. Said Mr. Atteberry:

"My father was a lay minister . . . rough elements would occasionally attempt to disrupt the services. It was my father's policy on such occasions to leave the pulpit and walk down the aisle, grab the offender by the seat-of-his-pants and the scruff of the neck and throw him out on his ear . . . On another occasion my father happened to enter the front door of my grandfather's blacksmith shop just as a roughneck was directing abusive language at my grandfather. Dad again applied the seat-of-the-pants and neck holds, propelled the offender out the shop and walked him by this hold about half the length of the block and sent him on his way with the toe of his shoe.

"Still another time a large bully, who carried a long barreled six shooter was threatening an Englishman of 120 pound weight. Once again my father, about 60 pounds lighter than the bully, used the pants-neck method to wedge the bully between two bales of broomcorn so tightly he was completely immobilized."

Concluded Mr. Atteberry, "This old tried and proven method of removing offenders from trouble spots was a standard procedure of which not enough is being done. I commend the Ranger for his knowledge and use of this method."

Chris Dixie noted that in the previous year's injunction hearing, Captain Allee testified that he could not have held Dimas's face up to the moving freight cars because no train went by. Reminded that moments earlier in the federal case he had testified that a train in fact did pass by, Captain Allee said, "I don't know whether I made a mistake in that case. We all make mistakes."

Later, testifying on the arrest of Dimas and Rodriguez, Captain Allee said that while searching for the pair, he had followed in his car some union members who went to the rented house. Dimas, holding a gun, came out of union volunteer Kathy Baker's house. At that point Ranger Dawson turned on the car lights. "I could have killed Dimas if I wanted to, and maybe I should have," the captain said. "I could have shot him three or four times . . . I considered him a dangerous man because he had killed a man at Floresville."

Dimas ran back into the house shouting, "Don't shoot, don't shoot; I haven't got a gun!" He locked the door, and after he would not respond to demands to open it, Captain Allee, who had obtained a search warrant from Justice of Peace Lopez, kicked in the door and made the arrests. The Ranger captain said he hit Dimas on the side of the head with a shotgun after the union members had refused to rise from a table where they were sitting and place their hands atop the tables. "I could have broken his neck if I wanted to," he testified.

Under cross-examination, Captain Allee amended his statements about Dimas. He said that although he could have killed him, he really didn't want to.

Ranger Van Cleve testified that during the Mission incident he arrested Mrs. Krueger following the arrest of her husband because he thought she was going to hit Captain Allee with a camera she was carrying. Van Cleve said he did not slap Ed Krueger and denied saying, "You better shut up or I'll knock your block off," as had been brought out in previous testimony. He indicated that while he was driving a group of union sympathizers to be charged, he noted that Ed Krueger, who was in the back seat, kept leaning over the front seat. Van Cleve said he merely pushed the minister back "because he smelled bad." One of the valley papers, the Corpus Christi *Caller*, reported that Ed had been pushed back because "he had bad breath."

Ranger Dawson, who also testified, said that during the incident in Mission he removed a camera from Pancho Medrano, former Texas heavyweight boxing champion who works for the UAW citizenship department, "because I thought he was going to hit me with it." Later the Ranger said he opened the movie camera as well as another camera he also took from Medrano to check for possible concealed weapons. The cameras were loaded only with film, which was exposed, although Dawson said he opened them after dark.

To clear up another question, the Ranger said Doug Adair, Texas editor of *El Malcriado*, also was arrested after the final car had already passed through the town.

"Then how could he have done anything to impede the train?" inquired Judge Brown. Apparently the judge felt there was no case against Adair.

Later Gary Garrison, who covers the Rio Grande Valley for the Associated Press, said Adair was apprehended while standing a considerable distance from the right of way. The train, he said, had already passed out of sight. Garrison claimed a Ranger, whom he could

not identify, pointed to Adair and said to him, "You look
like you want to be arrested."

At the morning testimony, Starr County Chief Deputy
Raul Pena related that on January 26, 1967, he had arrested the Reverend James Drake of Delano, California,
and Gilbert Padilla, leader of the farm labor movement
in Texas, while the two were peacefully praying on the
courthouse grounds. They were charged with unlawful
assembly, which had been declared unconstitutional by
the Texas Supreme Court. Pena testified he heard "only
bad words" and no praying. A broadside was leveled at
Raul Pena by Judge Garza for delaying the granting of
bond to Eugene Nelson.

"You know Joe Guerra of Roma [who guaranteed the
two-thousand-dollar bond] is a good man," said Judge
Garza. "You know the mayor of Roma City. You know he
is wealthy and is good for two thousand dollars."

Pena replied his check of tax office records didn't
show that Guerra owned any property.

Starr County Attorney Randall Nye interjected in the
proceedings to point out that the tax records show the
properties as belonging to the Guerra estate and that as
soon as it was established that one seventh of the estate
belonged to Guerra then Pena did grant bond.

"It worries me," said Judge Garza. "People have a
right to get out of jail, regardless of what their political
beliefs are, if they can make bond."

Raul Pena testified at one point that dances, featuring
live music and political rallies, had also been held on
courthouse grounds. Dixie pointed to the arrests of the
Reverend Drake and Padilla as examples of the Starr
lawmen discriminating in the application of laws.

The Starr deputy denied that he distributed copies of
La Verdad, a vehemently anti-huelga newspaper, from

the Starr County Courthouse. However, he did acknowledge that he received the paper, published in Corpus Christi, at the county offices, that he often made trips in a county automobile to pick up the newspaper at the bus station and that he carried copies of the publication in an official county car. But Pena re-emphasized that he did not distribute the newspaper.

On October 22, 1968, the bitter suit between the farm union (UFWOC) and the Texas Rangers had drawn to a close.

The suit against the Texas Rangers filed by the Texas Council of Churches alleging materially the same offenses as that of the UFWOC, AFL-CIO, was still pending early in 1969. It was not mandatory that the TCC's suit be held by a three-judge panel since the church group did not attack the constitutionality of Texas laws. As we shall see, the suit never came to trial because the Texas Council of Churches decided to compromise with law-enforcement officers and drop their charges. It was then that the Reverend Ed Krueger was fired.

In addition to the suits in the law courts, there were other hearings. The U. S. Civil Rights Commission held a hearing at which Captain Allee testified. The commission held early in July 1967, a week-long hearing on the problems of the Mexican-Americans in the Southwest. One of the facts revealed at the hearings came from Colonel Wilson E. Speir, head of the Texas Department of Public Safety. He was asked about the commission statistics that showed less than 2 per cent of the 1750 uniformed and plainclothesmen in the state highway patrol were Mexican-American. Speir said he didn't know why there "hasn't been very much interest shown by Mexican-Americans in employment by us."

Carlos Truan, a Corpus Christi insurance agent who

is a member of the Texas State Advisory Committee of
the U. S. Civil Rights Commission observed that "in
Starr County everybody and his brother-in-law is involved in a political situation that divides the community in half. You have the New Party and the Old Party
(both Democratic). Ironically enough the New Party
has been in power for over twenty years—so we can't
really say it is 'new' in that sense. It literally controls the
school system and everything else in the county. If you
want to get somewhere in Starr County you'd better
play ball with county officials and the New Party.

"A good example," Truan continued, "is the court
situation. There are some one hundred cases pending
against the farm workers. We asked Randall Nye, the
county attorney, why there were so many cases pending. He said, 'Well, I haven't been able to get together
with the attorney for the union.' But when we talked with
the union attorney, Jim McKeithan, he said he couldn't
get the cases tried.

"The farm workers complained that it was most difficult to get Mr. Nye to accept complaints brought by
the union. The excuse usually given by Nye was 'insufficient evidence.' On the other hand, the Texas Rangers
and the county officials had no difficulty in getting complaints accepted. For example, there was the case of one
woman who tried to file a complaint with Nye against
Jim Rochester, an official of La Casita. Rochester allegedly drove a bus into her while she was picketing outside La Casita. Nye refused to accept the complaint on
the grounds of 'insufficient evidence.' This woman, in-
cidentally, required medical treatment."

The workers have a point when they maintain that
every avenue for breaking through the rigid social structure they have known for generations has been cut off.

Another significant hearing was held on June 29, 1967, when the first official hearing of a committee of the United States Senate was convened in Rio Grande City. On that day the Senate Subcommittee on Migratory Labor heard testimony concerning the broadening of the workers under its provisions.

Senators participating in the inquiry included Chairman Harrison Williams of New Jersey, Edward Kennedy of Massachusetts and Ralph Yarborough of Texas. At the hearing witnesses described the difficulty of organizing farm workers into unions because of the absence of official procedures or guidelines by which labor and management could be brought to the conference table for mutual negotiations. They also testified about the employment of green-card commuters as scabs and the intervention of the Texas Rangers.

Captain Allee refused to testify before the Senate committee. After hearing testimony on the conduct of the Rangers, Chairman Williams noted that while "it is not the practice of this subcommittee to issue subpoenas . . . I would seriously consider issuing one for the appearance of Captain A. Y. Allee of the Texas Rangers. There has been a great deal of testimony that Captain Allee and the Rangers under his direction have trespassed upon private property, made numerous arrests without legal cause, used physical force far beyond that required to take a subject into custody, participated in acts of strike-breaking and committed other infringements of personal and property rights." Later, the Texas Department of Public Safety, under whom the Rangers operate, refused to allow Captain Allee to testify in further hearings in Washington.

Support for the inclusion of the farm workers in the NLRB was voiced by a spokesman for Archbishop Robert

Lucey of San Antonio, the Texas Council of Churches, speakers from the Texas AFL-CIO and Starr County Attorney Randall Nye.

After the first day of the Senate hearings, the senators moved over to Edinburg for further hearings. Here both Ed Krueger and his wife Tina testified as to the treatment they had received from law-enforcement agencies. Overflow crowds greeted the senators, and for those who did not understand English, simultaneous translation of the testimony was relayed in Spanish through loud-speakers positioned outside the Starr County Courthouse and Edinburg school.

In a closing statement summing up the impact of the two days of testimony, Senator Williams noted that it was the "most powerful testimony this subcommittee has ever received as to extending NLRA coverage to farm workers." Nevertheless, Congress has not acted on the various bills to include farm workers, and prospects seem unlikely during the Republican administration.

The hearings must have inspired the youth of the valley, though, for as we shall see, they began to chant everywhere, "Brown is beautiful!"

CHAPTER 9

Brown is beautiful

ED KRUEGER had a new image by the time he had gone through his experiences with the Texas Rangers. Up to that time he was considered shy, yet possessing a warm and friendly spirit. Even when he was serious, there was an infectious smile. But when the valley newspapers had reported his militant activities, Ed confessed to me, "You know, I have been made out to be so aggressive and militant that I am beginning to assume that stature."

At first, Ed was regarded by the Anglos as an easy-going social worker in the valley who avoided stepping on even an ant. Mexican-Americans had looked on him with suspicion. "Why should anyone want to jeopardize his reputation by looking after the needs of the poor?" was their attitude. But his being pushed around by the Rangers changed all this—Ed had become both a villain and a hero.

It was natural then when protesting Mexican-American junior and senior high school youth at Edcouch-Elsa began demonstrating and staged a walkout in favor of improved education that Ed Krueger was blamed by the

white and communications media. He was now referred
to as the "militant minister." There was logic for blaming
Ed—the reasons for the walkout were based on the principle he espoused in his contacts in the Mexican-American *colonias:* instilling in poor people a sense of community involvement. The young people knew what their
problems were and saw what was happening to their
parents and relatives. They decided to do something
about it.

When the young people of the high school asked for
a meeting with the board of education to discuss mutual
problems, the board found it more important to go hunt-
ing and to attend out-of-town football games.

Ed felt that the board was reacting with fear to the
increasing awareness of the Mexican-Americans regarding the level of education that is given in the Rio Grande
Valley. They seemed to think that to give in to the
students' demands would open the door to more ulti-
matums, such as bilingual education, more and better-
trained Mexican-American counselors who can relate to
the Chicano, Mexican-Americans in administrative positions, Mexican-American history courses and better attention to the problems of the migrant students.

On November 7, 1968, the students, now organized
as the Mexican-American Youth Organization (MAYO),
presented a series of demands to the Edcouch-Elsa officials and administrators. There were fifteen requests; one
can read between the lines and discover some of the
problems.

1. That no disciplinary action be taken against any
student or teacher who has taken part in this movement
and that all suspended students and teachers be rein-
stated in their posts or offices and that any mention of
such action be omitted from the school records.

2. That no threats, intimidation or penalties be made against any student for membership or attendance at any club or organization outside of school.

3. That the students be allowed to select their own candidates for Student Council; it should be a students' organization, not one of the students selected by the administration.

4. Excessive and unfair penalties and punishments stop for minor infractions and completely ridiculous reasons. For example, a student was suspended for three days for failure to stand at a pep rally. Or, if an item (shorts, tennis shoes) is stolen from the lockers, the students are punished (paddled or sent to do manual labor) for not being able to suit up.

No paddlings be given to a student until explanation for the punishment be given to parents if students request such explanation.

5. That no teacher or administrator use profanity or abusive language in the presence of students and in no case should a teacher lay a hand on a student in class.

6. That in the case of tardy or absent students, the student be allowed to reenter class and not have points taken off until his excuse is verified.

7. That either the cost of the cafeteria lunch be lowered to a more reasonable price or that more and better food be served.

8. That as Chicano students they be allowed to speak their mother tongue, Spanish, on school premises without being subjected to humiliating and unjust penalties.

9. That courses be introduced as a regular part of the curriculum to show contributions of Mexican-Americans and Mexicans to Texas and the Southwest region. For instance, factual accounts of the history of this state and

region, courses in Mexican history and culture. Also, that qualified, certified teachers be hired to teach these courses.

10. That all college preparatory courses be carefully explained to students by the time they enter high school.

11. That more effective counseling be given students from understanding counselors that are able to relate to students . . . Likewise there should be more assemblies on career opportunities, availability of scholarships, grants, loans, college entrance requirements, etc.

12. That the blatant discrimination against Mexican-Americans in this school stop immediately.

13. That regulations for "passes" be clearly defined so that no question remains as to when passes are needed. The present system is ridiculous.

14. That special attention be given the situation in which a great number of Edcouch-Elsa students find themselves; they are migrant workers themselves and children of workers. Students' choices of subjects in spring registration be respected and adopted in the fall term. Migrants leave school early so they take part in an accelerated program. Advance tests should be given to them before they leave for the north. This is often overlooked by teachers.

15. That school facilities be improved, renovated, replaced where appropriate. Teachers often use fans for their own comfort and ignore the students. Heaters are outdated, worn out and do not work at all. Some of the restrooms are not cleaned, fixtures are inoperable and constantly out of order. Broken windows are not replaced. There is no hot water for the showers. Holes in the walls should be filled and the outside of the buildings given a face lifting. We want to be proud of our school.

The students also scored the fact that school buses

were being driven by the teachers. The students wanted unemployed townspeople to fill such positions.

The response by the Establishment to the students' demands was not one of joy, to say the least. Rather the school board fell back on the old saw that they were in control of the school, not the students. When a meeting was finally arranged to hear the complaints, a room was chosen which could not accommodate interested citizens, the public-address system was inadequate so that no one could hear or understand what was taking place and the meeting was conducted in English so that the majority of those present could not understand the proceedings. No arrangements were made for any interpretations to be given in Spanish.

Said one of the students, "When the honorable, proper channels are closed to people, then the people have only one recourse, and that is to demonstrate their determination to seek redress of grievances through appealing to public opinion. The improvement that will come will benefit all of the community."

So two hundred students walked and demonstrated around the school and in the town. They carried signs which read, "Brown is beautiful," "Some of my best friends are Anglos," "Be a Christian today, take a Gringo out to lunch," and next to a palm tree against which a Mexican was taking a siesta a sign read, "When you see this sign, fight."

The valley newspapers were critical of the students' actions and the suspected involvement of Ed Krueger. Who else could have perpetrated such an exhibition? The youngsters were called racist agitators and trouble-makers by the white citizens and the unsympathetic newspapers.

One of the students told me, "I'd like to answer the

charge about being racist. People who call us that don't know the meaning of the word. Racism is a feeling of superiority. George Wallace loves his niggers as John Connally loves his farm workers. The white man is born with this disease. He has a feeling of superiority over his subjects. He laughs at our customs, traditions, language and history. He feels we ought to go to a vocational school but we do not need to go to college. The Anglos laugh at us when they portray our people sleeping beside a cactus or palm tree. They call us names like Frito Bandito and ridicule our dialect like referring to the telephone book's Jellow Pages."

Another student chimed in to point out that Mexican-Americans received more medals of honor in World War II than any other ethnic group and that Mexican-Americans have the highest percentile death rate and casualties in the Vietnam War.

The new breed of students does not have much patience with those who label them racist. They feel that such individuals are the real racists, for their idea of an American is a white Anglo-Saxon Protestant. To these students an American is one who is born in the United States, no matter what his color, creed, language or religion.

The young people have been able to comprehend the sham of white Americans. They know that whites in the valley have refused to accept Mexican-Americans as equals. Ed Krueger said to me one afternoon as we were on our way to a *colonia*, "The culture, traditions and language of these people is not acceptable to the whites—except when taught in some high school class up North. Down here we are trying to make whites out of Mexican-Americans; we want them to be like us."

The students want to learn English, but at the same

time they are proud of their heritage. They want a bilingual and bicultural society to exist and be supported in the valley.

I spoke with a group of students about the label pinned on them by some good valley church people that they are Communists. Even some of the clergy have harbored such thoughts.

"This shows they do not know what Communism is," said one young man. "If they would read the writings of Karl Marx, they would find out that in a Communist society the economics of a nation comes before the human needs of the people. So when they use our language, culture, traditions, they are twisting principles to serve their own ends."

Then one of the girls asked how the whites could reconcile the fact that they use Spanish in newspaper ads to sell their merchandise but do not want to teach Spanish as a second language in school.

"They do not want to pay the minimum wage," argued a perceptive student, "because the whites say they are not making enough money. But look where they live! See how they dress! Observe the kinds of cars they drive! We can only afford what they discard, and then they cheat us by telling how good it is. You know, 'It was driven by a little old lady who never took it out of the garage.' The whites know that half of our people earn less than three thousand dollars a year. They are lying about not having enough money. We are the ones who don't have enough for a decent living. These whites feed their pets more food than many of our families have in a day."

"We believe human needs come first; give us this," added another student.

To the charge of being troublemakers and agitators,

the students answer that when they see people living in poverty, people going up North because valley jobs are closed to them, 60 per cent of the students dropping out of school either because they have to work or because school does not hold their interest, when Mexican-Americans are stymied from getting top decision-making positions but always the "Yes, sir" or "No, sir" jobs, then they know that someone has to agitate to bring about change. These students are sensitive to the hollow expressions of their people. As one young person said, "When you try to rock the boat, you are making trouble for someone, and that is why they call us troublemakers. But they know that the history of the past has been changed in mines, mills and sweatshops by those who were called troublemakers in their time."

The students explained that MAYO members believe that their people have much to offer the nation. When I asked Ed Krueger about this, he pointed out that the young people are trying only to develop leadership among themselves. They feel it is essential for their people to have an awareness of what is happening in the areas of poverty, education and jobs. "This awareness will create action so that people can meet their problems and create new leadership."

Not all whites are inflicted with the "supremacy disease." The ones who do have it are called "gringos," in disdain. Some of the Anglos, like Ed, are held in high respect. Like him, they are willing to learn the language, to accept the culture and to go to jail with the Mexican-Americans. Friends are willing to listen to and follow the Mexican-American leaders.

Enemies, as the students see them, are the individuals who come into the "brown" communities and organizations and say, "Now we will handle the problem; don't you worry, we will take care of you."

"We believe that MAYO will make this county a better place to live in," said a teacher who had joined our little group. "They are hopeful that there will develop two strong groups in the valley—the Mexican-Americans and the Anglos—who will realize that they need each other. The final goal will be one people, but that will not happen until the white man starts to listen to the brown man and the black man and gives them control over their own lives."

This matter of education among Mexican-Americans has concerned many, especially Dr. Octavio Romano, professor at the University of California at Berkeley. "Do you know," he exclaimed, "that there are Mexican-Americans who have lived in this country twelve, twenty, thirty years who still do not command enough English for such simple things as 'go to hell, you bloodsucking vampire!'"

To remedy this linguistic problem, Professor Romano envisions a plan to set up language workshops throughout the Southwest in order to teach basic English to Spanish-speaking Mexican-Americans. With tongue in cheek, he says that the workshops will teach practical phrases which they need to use in their everyday lives. They can begin, for example, with such words as "pay me," "don't push me," "don't yell at me," "I want a raise" and "I quit."

As the student progresses in the linguistic training, says Professor Romano, he will be taught more complicated phrases: "pick your own damn crops," "investigate the Texas Rangers" and "fill out your own stinking questionnaire."

Finally, students will be encouraged to attempt more complicated English. They will be taught to say, "No, I'm not an informant. I am a consultant on Mexican-American life. Pay me" or "Obviously you are not acquainted with the fair-wage law of this county, you chiseling jackass."

"The situation is grave," says Romano, "and such workshops should go a long way toward solving the language problem of Mexican-Americans, even though much, much more research on Mexican-Americans is needed before we can come to a definite conclusion. Hopefully, someday Mexican-Americans will be able to speak English without an accent like Lady Bird Johnson or George Wallace."

One afternoon when Ed Krueger and I went out to visit a group of young people, I asked a Chicano to write me a piece on whom he considers himself to be. When I arrived home, he had mailed me his articulate reply. He was proud of his ancestors. "Now my ancestors came to this hemisphere from Western Europe. They came and met the other side of my family in Mexico—the Indians. They were a great race of people, a great culture. There were many kinds of Indians and Spaniards. They mixed, married, had children. These were called Mestizos. That is what I am."

Then he wrote, "We don't live in your neighborhood unless you call us Spanish, French or something else, but not what we are. We usually attend our own schools in the elementary or junior high and if we can get as far as high school, we may go with you. However, even before we finish high school more than 50 per cent of us are dropouts, and you know we don't go to college. We make up less than 1 per cent of the college students even though we are 12 per cent of the total school population. We don't use the government agencies because our experiences with them have been rather poor. They haven't been very friendly or helpful to us. We usually are Catholics and sometimes Protestants, but even here we have our own churches. Almost next door to each other there will be a Spanish church—Methodist or Catholic—and an Anglo church. You want us to stay away from you.

"When we attend your parties or meet your friends you introduce us as Spanish. You are ashamed of what we are, and thus, you make us ashamed; we don't think we are wanted. We seldom play sports, we are not nominated for student offices, we are not welcome at school dances, we aren't valedictorians at graduation, rarely are we given honors even in Spanish courses and we seldom are given leading parts in school plays.

"Who am I? They call me the forgotten one, chili snapper, taco, spic, mex, greaser. At the time of war you call me the great Patriotic American, during elections I am called by the politicians as 'the great Spaniard' but when I ask for a job, you refer to me as 'that damned Mexican.'

"Who am I? I am a human being. I have the same hopes that you do, the same fears, the same drives, the same desires, the same concerns, the same abilities. All I want is the same chance that you have as an individual. Who am I? In reality I am who you want me to be."

What can we say? It would be anticlimactic, but this one final point needs to be made. The college crowd, while in a small minority, at Pan American College in Edinburg have shown their support for the high school students. In what some call an underground newspaper, *M.A.Y.O. Pan Americano,* the November 1968, issue was "dedicated to the bravery of the Edcouch-Elsa students." Throughout the issue there are sprinkled illustrations of the thunderbird symbol of the National Farm Workers Organizing Committee, AFL-CIO, of Cesar Chavez and the revolutionary symbol of Zapata with its slogan *"Nosotros Vencaemos."* One of the articles shows a sketch of President Nixon along with a rat and the caption "Nixon eats grapes." The accompanying article tells the students about the California grape situation: "For us it is still 1930 and the 'Grapes of Wrath' are still growing . . . You can help by not buying California grapes until the strike is settled fairly. When you refrain from buying California grapes (except DiGiorgio and Hi Color) you are telling those growers that you do not wish to take the food from the mouths of children."

I asked Ed Krueger if he had anything to do with this paper. There was his usual laugh, a twinkle in his eye. "I suppose I am blamed for the actions of the students, but really these are young, liberal Mexican-Americans who are opening their eyes. I don't have anything to do with their work."

But, I thought to myself, who is helping to open their eyes? Who is organizing the *colonias* so that young men like Reynaldo de la Cruz, president of Colonias del Valle, made up of the representatives of all the *colonias*, can become a spokesman for valley residents?

CHAPTER 10

The *colonias* and what they are

DR. HAROLD KILPATRICK, the former executive secretary of the Texas Council of Churches felt that the emphasis of the valley ministry had to be, as he put it, on "the need to enlist these groups (those who are members of the Establishment) in the effort rather than fight them."

Ed, however, felt that it would compromise the program he and the TCC had established to subject it to dominant community structures. "We are trying to build leadership among the poor," he said, "so they can speak for themselves. Certainly their voice needs to be heard a lot more throughout the entire community and nation."

So Ed began to focus his efforts on organizing the poor in four counties—Hidalgo, Starr, Cameron and Willacy. He began in the *colonias,* which are the shantytowns where the families of the farm and other day laborers of some one hundred valley communities live. It is here that conditions are most deplorable. The *colonias* lack sewage systems, running water, good streets and other usually taken-for-granted facilities. Ed estimates that about ninety thousand Mexican-Americans in a region of approximately four hundred thousand population live in impoverished environments.

Ed believed that the poor themselves should develop leadership in the *colonias*. He visited the shantytowns, ferreted out the spokesmen, whether men or women, talked to them and then set up a meeting of the leaders. These individuals were then gradually trained and instructed in ways in which they might have influence on people outside the *colonias*, such as commissioners and political leaders.

"You can see why we need to help Mexican-Americans when you look at this ballot," he said. "I have a hard time myself in understanding it, so problems the uneducated have with it are fantastic." He pointed out the issues considered in the November 5, 1968, Texas general election when, besides voting for state officials, voters were asked to consider fourteen proposed constitutional amendments. "I think people in the *colonias* ought to be informed on these changes so they know exactly how their lives will be affected," he insisted.

Ed goes up and down the valley talking to the leaders and organizing them in the *colonias*, trying hard to keep the organizations from being "used" by a lot of people. "One of our roles is to protect the self-identity of the organizations, to protect them from the politicians and the well-meaning people, to keep them from using the *colonias* for their own purposes."

Food and clothing are distributed in the communities to needy families. The democratically elected *colonia* leaders find the families who are in desperate straits and see to it that their needs are met. Distribution of food and clothing is handled in each *colonia*, with some eight hundred families receiving assistance.

In addition to providing basic necessities, the *colonias*

are developing essential concepts—leadership ability, mutual understanding, respect for ideas and opinions of others, self-initiative, group planning and decision making, clear expression, mutual responsibility and recognition of the need to co-operate. "Added to this," said Ed, "is the joy of living and working in the community, the faith that problems can be solved and the experience that it is more blessed to give than to receive."

Symposiums, such as those held for three days in May 1968, bring together the leaders of the *colonias*. Along with national personalities and prominent Mexican-American professional people, the symposiums focus attention on issues affecting Mexican-Americans, consider quantity buying to lower food prices, build self-help housing and study such subjects as English and arithmetic. One important aspect considered is how to relate to established valley agencies, such as health boards. At the local meetings, topics of discussion relate to voter registration, job opportunities in other states and opinions regarding the schools.

Meetings of the *colonias* are open to both Mexican-Americans and Anglos. Ed feels that there is a "genuine atmosphere of good will, creative sharing, enthusiastic altruism and a good spirit of working together for the solution of common problems."

Some of the Anglos who have attended meetings of the *colonias* have been surprised at the quality of leadership and the eagerness of the Mexican-Americans to face squarely and explain their problems, to give their own resources including their cars, trucks, gas and time for working out transportation problems, to set up appointments for doctors, to look for wholesale prices, to pack boxes of donated food, to call and transport nurses who visit needy families. Said one enlightened

Anglo, following an evening meeting, "I have been impressed. Many of the old stereotypes and attitudes I had before I came tonight just seemed to fade away."

Ed finds that significant changes have taken place in the *colonias* and among the leaders. The group process has helped to identify potential leaders. Some of the ancient barriers have been eliminated. A new community spirit has been established along the valley in working with other *colonias,* and this "has brought out the best in individuals."

Most of the *colonias* pay a dollar-a-week dues to the incorporated organization made up of representatives of all the *colonias* and known as Colonias del Valle. This provides a central fund for gasoline, telephone, notices and emergencies.

One of the disappointments Ed has had is the seeming lack of interest of valley ministers in the *colonias.* "Ministers haven't been able to find time to visit in the *colonias* and to attend *colonia* meetings," he remarked. "I don't believe there is a very complete understanding of what goes on. I have invited the clergy and have asked them to go along with me, but none have accepted."

Probably the cause of the indifference of the clergy in this respect is due to the fact that few Mexican-Americans are made welcome in white churches. There is also suspicion and misinformation among the valley Establishment about the *colonias.* Conservative leaders in the valley like to refer to and link social programs with "anarchic movement."

Such references have caused the former Texas Council of Churches executives big "Excedrin headaches," particularly in regard to financial contributions. As Dr. Jesse D. Reber, the associate executive director of the TCC said at a VISTA hearing in Hidalgo County (page

16 of transcript), "I do think we need a very clear, definite statement about what has taken place. We must admit things which have gone wrong. Not only for the community but for one of our largest financial supporters who is asking for this statement."

So despite the assurances Ed has made that his work in the *colonias* is for the benefit of all, he has not received much support from the white leadership in the valley. Rather, they have accused Ed of being paternalistic toward Mexican-Americans, and they have cut off funds from the support of the Council of Churches and the valley ministry.

CHAPTER 11

The *colonias* and the churches

THE Starr County Establishment did not favor the publicity emanating from the strike in the fields or from the strike on the part of the school children. A negative reaction set in toward Ed Krueger and the former Texas Council of Churches (TCC). The strike had been modest in its demands, and it involved few people. But the politicians, bankers, real estate agents, chamber of commerce and clergy were outraged. Oddly enough, these groups should have been the very ones to be pleased over the efforts of the Mexican-American to lift himself above starvation wages and to better his living and community standards.

The big problem with the Establishment was that any general plans or sudden uplifting of the Mexican-Americans in south Texas, of which the Starr County strike was a preliminary move, would be unsettling to the interests of the Establishment, which in turn, are the interests of the action culture itself. Thus it is that a proper Establishmentarian could well become unhinged by such a thing as a farm workers' strike.

As we have seen, the Texas Establishment worked very

hard to defeat the strike. Once they had done this, they cast a suspicious eye on the work of Ed Krueger among the *colonias*. Even the Texas Council of Churches began to feel the pressure. It ordered Krueger to put more emphasis on work with valley churches and ministerial groups. The council organized a service committee made up of two to four representatives of each principal church body in the valley. But polarization had set in and many people were convinced that the TCC was interested only in farm workers and that it was highly partisan regarding labor-management issues.

The Establishment looked askance at Ed Krueger's working among the Mexican-Americans in the *colonias*. There are one hundred of these unincorporated communities in the lower Rio Grande Valley. Those who are in the know have conjectured that the poverty in these small villages is as severe as anywhere else in the country, and some of it is as bad as the situation just across the border in Mexico.

Most of the people who live in the *colonias* are seasonal farm workers. What did Ed find when he began to check out the conditions of these people? The Office of Economic Opportunity (OEO) came up with some interesting information relative to four valley counties— Cameron, Hidalgo, Starr and Willacy.

There are 372,123 people in these counties, 254,766 of whom have Spanish surnames. Of the families here, 38,924 have an income of less than three thousand dollars a year, and 11,225 families make less than one thousand dollars; 27,669 have an income between one thousand and three thousand dollars a year.

There are 36,363 females over fourteen years of age who are working in these four counties, and 81,658 males over fourteen. Of the 160,000 of the population who are twenty-five years old and older, over half have less than an eighth-grade education.

Of 100,059 housing units in the four counties, 45,667 are substandard. Out of these houses come 2201 young people examined for Selective Service. Of this number 1152 were rejected because of poor health and failure to meet educational standards. Even then, most of those called to duty from the aforementioned counties have been Mexican-Americans.

Ed found that the average life expectancy of the people is forty-nine years. The death rate of the farm worker as a per cent of the national rate is:

Infant mortality
   125% higher than the national rate
Maternal mortality
   125% higher than the national rate
Influenza and pneumonia
   200% higher than the national rate
Tuberculosis and other infectious diseases
   260% higher than the national rate
Accidents
   300% higher than the national rate

Having these statistics at hand, Ed decided that he might best serve in the valley as an organizer within the *colonias*. He would develop the leadership among the Mexican-Americans so that they could exert some pressure on the society that surrounds them.

Ed and I visited many of these *colonias*. I could tell that his work was cut out for him. Most of the slum clusters reeked with poor sanitation and disease. Roads were dusty and rutted. One home I visited, in which there

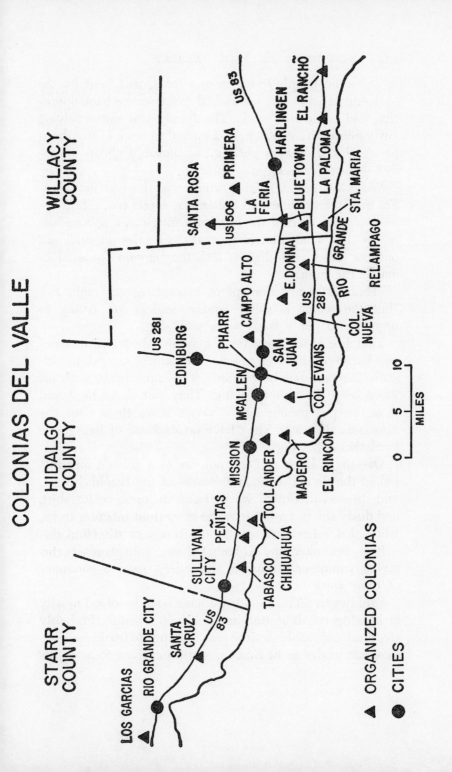

COLONIAS DEL VALLE

were eleven people living in one room, was built on the back end of a lot. The father had had a severe back operation and could not work. The family was not receiving any welfare, so the older children had to work in Edinburg for Anglos who were getting unbelievably cheap labor—five dollars for a night's work.

We drove past a *colonia* which was deemed first-class. For nearly four thousand dollars, an Anglo real estate developer was offering the Mexican-American a 24×24-foot house on a small plot of ground. As a sales gimmick, an outdoor toilet was thrown into the bargain "painted to match the house."

"There is one water spigot in each house," said Ed, "but the water is salty. So the leaders are trying to organize to get a fresh-water well dug."

That life is not easy for the valley Mexican-American was borne out by a law man. "We protect our white citizens. They are our best people. They are always with us. They keep the county going. They put us in here and they can put us out again, so we serve them. But the Mexicans are trash. They have no standard of living. We herd them like pigs."

One night Ed and Tina took me to a *colonia* meeting. I shed the tie and coat, trademarks of the Establishment, and dressed in brown work slacks, an open white shirt, and dusty shoes. I went into the store-front meeting room, where Ed introduced me to the board of directors.

Paul Brubaker and Duane Gibson, college graduates giving volunteer service to the valley, gave a summary of their work.

Paul began, "This month we have been involved mostly in housing rehabilitation and self-help housing. Probably the most enjoyable project was helping Pedro Pena Flor, a *colonia* leader in El Rincon, add a bedroom to his little two-room house. Construction materials were made available through an FHA (Federal Housing Authority) loan. Mr. Pena Flor did most of the construction, asking our assistance in building the rafters and the roof." The report also revealed that in many *colonias,* the film, in Spanish, *Six Houses, Six Homes* was shown three or four times a week. The film explains how families can obtain government loans and can enter into a community self-help housing program.

Duane told how an interesting part of the work has been relating the valley situation and *colonia* life to several visitors to the area. He had spent most of one day with a photographer from the United States Commission on Civil Rights.

"After a good look at the *colonias,* we visited the Reynosa Bridge at 5:30 one morning to see hundreds of green-card workers coming to the United States for agricultural work. This was a special interest, knowing that the day before we talked to *colonia* men who were unable to find employment in the fields. It was evident that the green-card workers were taking jobs away from our Mexican-American citizens."

After Duane and the photographer had taken a few pictures, a customs agent threatened them, saying, "Do you realize that it is against the law for you to take pictures in a port of entry without permission! You are violating the law and can be fined."

Duane and the photographer had their cameras taken from them. The port director had said to them that they "should not get mixed up" with this labor dispute. Several days later, the two men found that their film had been exposed. Duane's camera was damaged to the extent of forty-three dollars.

"This whole story," explained Duane, "only shows that

even many government employees, whom one would think would be for helping the American public, are able to use their power and influence in protecting what is right in their own eyes. Many of these people seem very prejudiced and against any activity of social change. If we are not involved in change, this tells the world that we are in favor of the present situation."

Ed gave a monthly summary of his work from September 10, 1968, to October 15, 1968. He pointed out that the one item which occupied more time than any other single item was the service leadership-development projects.

His work for the reporting period included:

Eleven evening meetings in *colonias*

Four meetings of the board of directors and executive committee of Colonias del Valle

One meeting of the Cameron County Community Action Agency (CAA)

One meeting with representatives of Hidalgo CAA in regard to placement and program of VISTA

Seven conversations with ministers with additional contacts with lay leaders

One VISTA program committee meeting

Talks with visitors to the valley—government and church leaders

One meeting of the National Migrant Health Review Committee

One meeting with Farmers' Home Administration Office in Temple, Texas

Many visits to *colonias* and talks with their leaders

One of Ed's involvements included his association with the Volunteers in Service to America, commonly called

VISTA, a federally funded program. In May 1968, when the Texas Council of Churches agreed to sponsor the VISTA Minority Mobilization program in Hidalgo County, Ed became involved by the nature of the work.

The valley ministry, of which Ed was an integral part, had as its purpose to (1) call the attention of the churches to the fact that in a rapidly changing society there is a constant need within the church for renewal, (2) be an agent of the church through which it might make a united witness and render a service to the people of several communities, (3) administer relief as may be available and such social services as resources permit to the needy of several communities, (4) assist disadvantaged people to achieve the know-how and strength in order to enter into creative competition to secure for themselves the inalienable rights of life, liberty and pursuit of happiness, (5) serve as a channel through which the churches outside the valley might express their love and compassion to the people of the valley and through which they might render such ministries and services as they might be able to make (6) and encourage the churches of the valley to establish an ecumenical agency or agencies so that these churches could unite in serving the community.

For nearly fifty years the Texas Council of Churches had been involved in the valley ministry covering Cameron, Hidalgo, Starr and Willacy counties. The function of Ed Krueger and other members of the staff was also clearly defined. Guided by the purposes already stated, they were to stimulate and assist people, particularly those living in *barrios* and *colonias,* to imitate and conduct positive enterprises, including individual and group enterprises that would lead to community development, contributing to the solution of their own problems by mutual assistance, leadership training and joint communications with other community agencies, both public and private.

In order to fully achieve this development, earnest effort was made to involve representatives of business, the professions or other interests of the community. Many of these representatives had invested time, talent and financial resources to improve the conditions of the people. The awareness and involvement of the total community would lead to a lasting Christian community. A second goal was to work with public and private agencies in health education, basic and vocational education and whatever means available to enable people to acquire skills for productive employment in business and industry as well as in agriculture.

A third goal was to serve as contact persons to enlist people in job-training opportunities and employment either within or outside the several communities in the valley. Still other goals of Ed's valley ministry were to administer relief funds and commodities, working through the churches and community organizations of the valley for referral and screening. He sought to maintain a liaison with churches along the border in Mexico, encouraging dialogue between the Anglo and Mejicano churches and communities for the purpose of improving mutual understanding, fellowship and enrichment, and of promoting programs, projects and organizations for the purpose of finding increasingly greater unity.

With these purposes and goals in mind, Ed found himself involved in social-action programs—not too acceptable in a conservative area such as the valley. He encountered and worked on problems of unemployment, low wages, inadequate diet, crowded and inadequate housing, lack of water, sewage, sanitation and drainage problems, sickness and infant mortality, illiteracy, high interest rates, high prices in stores, language barriers in school, lack of bilingual teachers and a host of other concerns. One can readily see that these problems were mostly the result of poverty. So Ed and the VISTA volunteers embarked on a program to enhance community life and to help the people in poverty become effective in dealing with problems that influenced their lives. This included the development of human resources, avoidance of paternalism, the encouragement of self-help and the involvement of individual Mexican-Americans in solving community problems.

I have gone into detail to spell out these goals and functions, showing how specific they were. This motivation gave Ed a positive direction in which to proceed. With the help of VISTA, he began establishing buyers' clubs and organizing citizenship classes, baby clinics, recreation programs, loan funds, self-housing, credit unions and legal-defense programs.

As Ed worked on the problems facing Mexican-Americans, the Establishment began to show resistance. They refused to acknowledge the existence of any problem at all so far as they were concerned. Therefore, no "solution" was necessary or possible. In the past, Mexican-Americans had been content with "tokenisms," but Ed began to change this. As these changes occurred, rumblings began to be heard in the valley. It was not another hurricane Beulah, but instead a movement to dump the Texas Council of Churches, the VISTA program and Ed Krueger.

The Reverend William A. Triggs, pastor of the United Methodist Church in Pharr and a member of the board of the Texas Council of Churches, began to feel the pressure of the Establishment who belonged to his church.

Mr. Triggs said that he was told the VISTA volun-

teers would be in the valley solely to help the under-
privileged "reach a state of self-determination through
education and organization," that they would have nothing to do with organized labor and that the Hatch Act
forbade them, as federal employees, to enter into any
political struggle. Mr. Triggs said he voted for sponsorship but that "almost immediately the young volunteers
were involved in squabbles with the Mission school system and with the city commissioners of Weslaco over the
location of a new swimming pool.

"Then came the national elections [1968]," he said,
"and suddenly my office was swamped with telephone
calls, with reports of VISTA being involved in various
political intrigues." That, plus the Edcouch-Elsa student
walkout, which saw nearly two hundred Mexican-American youth strike against the school system, was too much
for Pastor Triggs. He called for a clean sweep of VISTA
from the valley.

Jose Uriegas, whom Triggs wanted removed from the
VISTA program, answered the charges of the pastor relative to the involvement in the Edcouch-Elsa affair. "Two
students were reprimanded for not making enough noise
at a pep rally, then were expelled for three days for making too much noise at the next rally. This created a real
reaction among the students."

A week later, explained Jose, there was a meeting of
the Catholic Youth Organization, at which the special
guest was a representative from the National Student
Association, invited by the students to speak on bilingual
education. During his talk, the speaker began to speak
in Spanish, at which two Anglo teachers and a Mexican-
American school administrator protested. After a heated
discussion, the meeting was called off.

VISTA's participation in the entire movement cen-

tered around the informing of the entire community
about the demands of the students which were going to
be made public. The volunteers felt that as a community
developmental organization it should solicit community
involvement since this was a positive engagement.

The Texas Council of Churches was in hot water too.
A feeble attempt was made to more clearly define the
relationship it had with VISTA and Ed Krueger's Valley
Service Committee. But the attempt failed, and the council withdrew as a sponsor.

The hassle settled around three VISTA supervisors
whom almost everyone in the valley connected with the
Establishment, including the Reverend Billy Triggs,
wanted dropped. Jose Uriegas, VISTA project director for
the county, Merle Smith, deputy director, and David
Lopez, senior supervisor, were accused of "militant" activities. However, VISTA regional director Edward De La
Rosa refused to fire them.

The Establishment received help from Texas Republi-
cans in their effort to drop VISTA. Mrs. Polly Lowell of
McAllen, state deputy vice-chairman of the Republican
party, told the local press after a trip to Austin that she
hoped the volunteer program involving individuals
among Mexican-Americans would be scrapped.

Whenever the press reported on VISTA's work, it
would usually involve Ed in a detrimental way. Hoyt
Hager, a valley newspaperman, wrote of a meeting with
executives of a county community-action agency, "The
Rev. Ed Krueger was active a year ago in the melon
picketing in Starr County." Another valley writer, Virginia
Armstrong, wrote under a by-line "VISTA Boys Need
Haircuts," and that "newly arrived volunteers haven't
given any evidence yet that they're backing an organized
effort in McAllen to agitate, but an incident here and

there does indicate they must be looking about with a critical eye."

Apparently two of the young people wondered why it was so difficult for the poor to get a street light in the Mexican-American *barrios*. They went to see McAllen's city commissioner, Ralph Flores.

In the July 28, 1968, issue of the *Monitor*, Miss Armstrong wrote:

"Two long-haired youths walked in to announce they had some matters about the city to discuss with him. Some people were being neglected, they said.

" 'Who?' demanded Flores.

" 'A lot of people,' was the answer by the VISTA youths.

"Flores then told them that getting a street light isn't difficult. It costs the city only $3 a month, he said, to pay for the electricity, and almost anyone who asks automatically gets results."

After a telephone call from Flores to the assistant city manager, Don Sisson, the commissioner said no requests had been made by anyone for a light at the intersection under discussion.

Then he had a suggestion, according to the newspaper account. If the youths planned to stay around McAllen and hoped to do anything effective, their next stop should be to go to get haircuts and spruce up.

Several days later VISTA volunteers attended a meeting of the city commission. They asked Mayor Paul Veale why the governing body met in the afternoons. He explained that by meeting late in the afternoon, the commission members could get in a full day's work at their businesses and still have the evenings with their families. But young people today are sharp and see through adult hypocrisy. They knew that evening meetings were not held because then the poor could attend and make their requests.

The young volunteers were stirring up a hornets' nest all over McAllen. They were accused of picking out the poorest neighborhoods and plunging in to solve their problems. The fact that the VISTA office was located in San Juan in the same building as was occupied by Ed Krueger's Valley Service Committee of the Texas Council of Churches did much to make the affluent look askance at the "long-haired volunteers." It was decided by the Establishment that the volunteers and Ed Krueger must go. They did not want anyone "to develop responsible local leadership through instilling in the poor people a sense of community involvement."

Said Jose Uriegas, "We don't know how to fix broken water pumps and things like that. What we do know is how to find the official responsible for seeing that it is fixed. You might say we are experts at helping the people find the experts." The poor are assisted in taking their problems to the officials who have the authority to do something about the problems. Some public officials would welcome this objective, but not those in power along the Rio Grande Valley.

The Establishment and private citizens did not mind volunteers doing referral work such as described by a VISTA supervisor. "There was a woman in Mission with a retarded child, who simply had no idea what to do with him. We found an agency which was willing to help her." Participation in such service tasks as staying with elderly people during an illness and doing small jobs that were beyond the reach of the poor in Hidalgo County was approved. The private citizen appreciated this kind of aid. But he disliked the field work of the volunteers that involved making house calls in poor neighborhoods, discussing problems that irked the poor, organizing discussions and showing directions in which to proceed—these were regarded as political activities and were "forbidden."

Ed Krueger continued with his plans for community development amidst a rising crescendo of hush-hush opposition. "Our goal," he said, "is to help the people find the means to help themselves." He was working on a number of self-help projects, such as the one in Barrio del Puerto, a settlement just outside Brownsville in Cameron County.

"It is amazing," he said, "how eager the people are to improve their lot. These stereotypes we use to label Mexicans—'If they're poor, it's just because they don't want to work,' 'If they really wanted a job, they could get one,' 'They're just looking for handouts' and 'The Mexican-Americans just don't want to work'—these are all hogwash."

Krueger told me that "it does not take a profound observer to see how the poor are left out. They need representation." Ed had attended a meeting at the Weslaco town hall and a commisssioner's court session in Cameron County. In both instances he was with VISTA volunteers and the poor.

Krueger has always felt very strongly about the need for people from the poor segment of the valley society to become involved in the issues which affect them. Out of this concern was organized the Colonias del Valle, or community groups, whose purpose was to develop neighborhood leadership in self-improvement programs. The service committee has been aiding the *colonias* in getting such a commonplace commodity as water. "Some of the people," said Ed, "are still carrying water from polluted canals."

But Ed's days of association with the Texas Council of Churches were numbered. The pressure was on not only to dump VISTA but also to dump Ed. The Texas Council had decided to withdraw from the sponsorship of the VISTA volunteers. However, Walter Richter, area director of the Office of Economic Opportunity, asked the council to reconsider, and after long negotiations, it resumed sponsorship with control assigned to the council itself. When the smoke of battle had cleared, Edward De La Rosa, regional head of VISTA, promoted David Lopez to project director of Hidalgo County, made Jose Uriegas director of south Texas and moved Merle Smith up in the state organization as deputy to Uriegas. The newspapers were furious over the turn of events, headlining the action as "Three VISTA workers booted up, not out."

The Establishment took a dim view of Ed's ministry in the valley, and some in the power structure meant to do something about it.

Scott Toothaker, an attorney in McAllen, Texas, and a member of the firm of Ewers, Toothaker, Ewers, Abbot and Evans, wrote February 1, 1968:

"This is being written to you and all other lay members of the Annual Conference of the Methodist Church in the McAllen District.

"As a member to the Annual Conference from St. Mark Methodist Church of this city, I am deeply concerned about a problem which I think all active church members should be acquainted with.

"Most Methodist churches are now preparing their annual budgets, and I assume that as usual your church budget will contain an apportionment for the Interdenominational Cooperation Fund, about one third of which goes to the Texas Council of Churches.

"During the past year, the Texas Council has maintained at least one representative in Starr and Hidalgo Counties. This individual, a Reverend Krueger, participated very actively with the agitators in the farm labor strife and turmoil that existed in Starr County for several months. Because of my representation of several of the people involved in that strife, I am intimately acquainted with many things that took place. The entire community of Rio Grande City was descended upon by a group of ruffians and agitators who openly, through newspapers and radio, vowed that no growing crops would move out of this area even if they had to burn bridges and use any other force, legal or illegal.

"The Texas Rangers were called in and, as a result, they used no more force than was necessary to maintain law and order. It should be remembered that one of these leaders of this movement was a known ex-convict and at that time he was out on parole for a second offense. All of these facts were well known by the law enforcement officers at the time they were dealing with him. This individual has since been arrested in Mexico and charged on Marijuana charges. Another one of the leaders has recently been arrrested and indicted on narcotics charges in Bexar County, Texas. These men were among the leaders of the group that the Texas Council of Churches was 'ministering to' and closely cooperating with.

"The farmers were able to harvest their crops, and these lawless ruffians were prevented from committing many of the crimes they had threatened.

"The Texas Council of Churches has seen fit to become deeply involved in this matter to the extent that it has retained attorneys and has filed suit (Cause No. 67-B-44, in the U. S. District Court for the Southern District of Texas, Brownsville Division) against the Texas Rangers,

charging them with, among other things, violating the
civil rights of several of those who participated in the
labor activities in Starr County. It is my opinion that
had the Texas Rangers not come into the area and enforced the law as they did, we would have had rioting,
the burning and destruction of property and possible loss
of life as the result of those who were terrorizing the community.

"I understand that the Texas Council is currently contributing very substantially to a fund known as the 'Valley Service Committee' and that its same representative,
Edwin (sic) Krueger, is back in this area and is getting
ready to renew this campaign in behalf of the Texas
Council.

"I think it is a disgrace when church funds, so des-
perately needed for so many worthwhile Christian causes,
are allowed to be used by any organization to enjoin
and suppress the enforcement of the laws of this state,
and I earnestly urge you to pray, as I have, about this
matter and recommend to your budget committee and
congregation that no funds from your church ever again
be forwarded to the Texas Council of Churches.

"If there is any additional information you would like
to have, I would be glad to furnish it to you.

Sincerely yours,
(*signed*)
Scott Toothaker"

In the meantime, a new face had entered the picture
in the person of Jesse D. Reber, associate secretary of the
Texas Council of Churches. He had previously served with
distinction as secretary of the Pennsylvania Council of
Churches, retired and moved to Texas to assist the exec-

utive director, Harold Kilpatrick. Mr. Reber's portfolio included the supervision of Ed's valley ministry.

Friction developed almost immediately between Reber and Krueger. Reber wanted to approach the Mexican-American problem through existing institutions, the power structure of the Establishment. We have already noted Ed's approach, through the poor and powerless.

On January 24, 1969, the issue reached a head. Ed's wife Tina had been in the hospital, and he was bringing her home when he saw the mailman a few doors up the street. He waited for him. Included in his mail was a letter from Harold Kilpatrick of the Texas Council of Churches.

"With the recommendation of the Personnel Committee I have the unpleasant duty to inform you that your tenure as a staff member of the Council is to be terminated as of February 24, 1969. However, a check for the full month of February is enclosed.

"As I had indicated to you in our conference of December 19, all staff members are being asked to resign as of the February 24 date because the Texas Council of Churches is scheduled to cease to function at that time. Doubtless some of the staff will be retained by the new organization at least for an interim but after a very detailed and careful evaluation of the Valley Ministry, officers and staff of the Council have decided that it is imperative to change not the general direction but the mode of conduct in important aspects of the Ministry.

"The churches of the Valley, both Anglo and Mexican-American, must become bases of field operations and task force units (with help from judicatories and councils) and we are convinced that under existing circumstances, you are not the man to direct this kind of campaign against discrimination, deprivation, and related ills. This statement in no way is intended to downgrade or show lack of appreciation for your dedicated service in the organization of colonias, massive relief efforts following Beulah, and the personal relation of you and Mrs. Krueger with scores of needy persons. I shall always respect and admire you for such dedication.

"It is good personnel practice, backed by our own experience, that when an employment is being terminated, it is best the departing employee be relieved of his duties as soon as possible, freeing him for making personal adjustments. Therefore, unless there is a real obstacle to do so, I request that you plan to remove personal effects and clear the Valley office at the close of business on Monday, January 27.

"I hope that you will join us in trying to make this transition as little disruptive as possible in the program to which you have given so much.

Sincerely,
(*signed*)
Harold Kilpatrick"

Ed Krueger had been fired!

CHAPTER 12

Repercussions from Krueger's dismissal

A VALLEY newspaper described Ed Krueger's dismissal as "militant minister of the Texas Council of Churches migrant ministry in the Rio Grande Valley has been fired."

Ed had three days from the time he received Harold Kilpatrick's letter on January 24, 1969, to clear up his personal effects and straighten out affairs in the valley ministry office. By the end of the day on January 27 he had to be out. When the news of Ed's dismissal hit the leaders of the *colonias* and the news wires, things began to happen.

The Texas Council of Churches, through its personnel committee under the chairmanship of the Reverend Carl Burkle, United Church of Christ Conference Minister from Austin, issued a memo giving the reasons for Ed's dismissal:

"1) Failure to maintain harmonious relations with the staff. Mr. Krueger failed to maintain proper relations with the executive staff and had been at serious odds with a coworker on the Valley staff.

"2) Failure to manifest interest in relating to our member churches in the Valley and pursuing a persistent course of alienating the very persons and institutions that could help achieve the goals of the Valley Ministry.

"3) Mr. Krueger declined to work under the policies and administrative regulations established by the Texas Council of Churches [described in the previous chapter]. More than that, on several occasions his activities were insubordinate to the administration of the Council. This obviously could not be tolerated by any staff."

"No one accused Ed of not diligently doing his job with the disadvantaged," Dr. Kilpatrick said. "He didn't relate to the staff or the churches of the valley. We saw after two years that we just couldn't get him to do it and that we would have to change our methods, not our goal."

Dr. Kilpatrick admitted that pressures had built up. "Ed and the VISTA volunteers just went too far out in planning things," he said. "They made a lot of trouble in conducting protests at city council and school board meetings.

"We tired of fighting city hall, courthouses, school boards and things that look like the Establishment," continued Dr. Kilpatrick. "We want to make use of those people. Ed was unwilling to change his strategy, so all we could do was let him go."

Some of the staff members in the valley contradicted the charges leveled against Ed. They declared that the charge that Krueger was at odds with other staff members was an exaggeration; that, at first, some difficulties arose, but that these were due to the lack of a clear-cut definition of responsibilities. Once this was cleared up, "Ed was easy to work with."

Members of the valley ministry also said that Ed was not directed specifically to relate to the churches in the valley until months after he was on the job. Then he did speak at churches and meetings, relating and interpreting the role of the valley ministry. However, people did not want to hear about changes in the political structure; church people were listening for requests that would give them some place to send their used clothing and their Thanksgiving and Christmas food baskets. So Ed was not successful in the local churches. Sides had already been taken.

When Jesse D. Reber, the associate secretary of the Texas Council of Churches, was asked to comment on the contradictions, he replied that there "absolutely" was a "serious" interstaff feeling of ill will and that he "knew" what he was talking about. "Krueger was fired for insubordination; he could not fit into any administrative supervision. Trouble was with the leaders who had come into the valley. A lot of people are just crusaders and that's all they want," he concluded.

Dr. Reber, who is a tough-minded seventy-one-year-old veteran with more than two decades in the service of ecumenical work among churches, mostly in Pennsylvania, made it clear following Ed's firing that he "will tolerate no militant foolishness from the TCC staffers in the lower Rio Grande Valley." In spelling out his new philosophy for the valley, he indicated there would be no room for picket signs, cries of "*huelga*" or pitched battles with the Texas Rangers.

"We intend to work through the churches in the area," he said, "and to orient our activities to the forces of reconciliation rather than to the polarization that sets people against people.

"Krueger simply wouldn't buy this," he added. "He became insubordinate and Dr. Kilpatrick fired him. Frankly, I would have fired him a year before Kilpatrick did had he been on my staff in Pennsylvania."

Such comments as these were "eaten up" by the conservative valley press. The remarks probably brought a great deal of joy to the Establishment as well.

Ed Krueger admitted to me that he has been highly critical of the TCC for appointing Dr. Reber to supervise the work of the valley ministry among the Mexican-Americans.

Reber was named without the consultation of the people in the valley. He had not had any association with the Mexican-Americans and early in his work indicated the direction he would be taking. At a meeting in Weslaco which Ed attended, Dr. Reber was speaking to a group of conservative laymen and local ministers. The meeting had taken place shortly after the Edcouch-Elsa school incident.

"Reber," said Ed, "was conciliating and apologetic in his approach." Then Ed told of a remark that Reber made that shocked and disgusted him. According to Ed, Dr. Reber said, "You wouldn't want Mexican-Americans in your church any more than you want Negroes. They are loud, smell bad and use foul language."

I asked Ed if he was sure Dr. Reber had said this. "Have you taken his remarks out of context, Ed?" I inquired.

"No," was the reply. "He said these things and added other stereotypes that I have forgotten. But after he made these statements there wasn't any further discussion of them."

The conflict that arose between Ed and Dr. Reber became the *modus operandi*. Dr. Reber did not go with Ed to any of the *colonias* or to *colonia* meetings. Soon after Dr. Reber arrived in Texas, he announced, after visiting the valley, that he would open an office in San Juan, install air conditioning and carpet the room.

While the executives and leaders of the Texas Council of Churches kept insisting that Ed was fired for insubordination, probably because of the gulf that existed between him and Dr. Reber, still another matter was influential in the motivation for Ed's dismissal. On December 20, 1968, Harold Kilpatrick had written a letter to Ed in which he said, "Several weeks ago I understood that Bishop Pope [United Methodist Bishop W. Kenneth Pope, presiding officer of the TCC] had been conferring with you about joining him as Council president in signing a compromise agreement withdrawing the suit against the Texas Rangers and certain Starr County peace officers, along with the signature of Colonel Pat Speir, Ranger commandant. In fact, I thought the agreement had been signed quite some time ago."

Ed told me that he had been called by telephone several times by Bishop Pope's office.

Dr. Kilpatrick's letter continued, "I talked to Bishop Pope by telephone a day or two ago and learned that no signatures had been obtained. He signed several copies, furnishing some to the attorney general's office for obtaining Colonel Speir's signature. Bishop Pope told me that the state officials wanted your signature and that of your wife but that it would not be necessary to obtain the Moreno and Becerra signatures . . .

"We hope to issue a press release immediately upon the rendering of a verdict in the farm union cause giving the background of the agreement. Therefore, it is desirable to have all signatures before this is done."

The compromise agreement that Ed and Tina were asked to sign was a revised text which made no reference to the Rangers' history or that of the council. The first draft had proved unacceptable to the attorney general's office. The revised agreement read in part:

"During the summer of 1967 a series of events occurred in the lower Rio Grande Valley which culminated in the filing of a lawsuit styled *Texas Council of Churches, et al vs. A. Y. Allee, et al,* Civil Action No. 67-B-44 in the United States District Court for the Southern District of Texas, Brownsville Division . . .

"All the parties to this lawsuit are desirous of bringing the lawsuit to a peaceful conclusion without fixing blame thereof. It is the hope of all that this controversy may be terminated peacefully so as to assure public confidence and good will to all concerned.

"The individually named parties to this lawsuit are but instrumentalities concerned with furthering the expressed purposes of the two named organizations with which each may be associated, either directly or indirectly. And none of these individuals would care to perpetrate this lawsuit to the detriment of either organization by calling strife or dissension where neither should exist.

"It is hereby declared to the purpose of all parties to this lawsuit, as well as the organizations they represent, that in the future they shall regard each other with faith and good will, and that they will exert every effort to carry out their objectives with honor and integrity.

"Wherefore, premises considered, it is agreed by each of the parties signatory hereto that Cause No. C. A. 67-B-44 . . . be dismissed by Plaintiffs at their cost with prejudice to the refiling of same and each Plaintiff signatory hereto hereby releases each and every Defendant herein from any liability growing out of the activities in said lawsuit."

One hitch developed in the otherwise nicely worded document. Krueger was asked to sign the agreement which had been approved by the Texas Rangers, but Ed refused to do so. He called the compromise statement inappropriate because it "would exonerate the Rangers from any blame" in the handling of himself, his wife and the farm workers, many of whom were faced with charges of violating state picketing laws and "are guilty until proven innocent."

Ed, who had been called "the only pastor the poor have ever had," also noted that the statement would prejudge the filing of suits against the Rangers in the future.

"That is a little too much to ask," said Ed. "I'm concerned about forgiveness and entering into new relationships, but I can't pretend that things didn't happen which did."

Krueger also said that the signed agreement might prejudice a case filed against the Rangers by the United Farm Workers Organizing Committee. That suit, still pending at the time, challenged the validity of state picketing laws.

Despite Ed's decision regarding the compromise agreement, Bishop Pope issued a statement to the press that "the lawsuit of the Texas Council of Churches involving certain grievances as a result of an incident occurring over a year ago in the Rio Grande Valley is being dropped by this body. Officials of the Texas Council of Churches feel that the purpose of the lawsuit has already been served in making known their complaints and in the assurance they have had that any such grievances will not be repeated."

With Ed's refusal to sign the agreement came an almost complete reversal of the TCC's regard of Ed Krueger. When the blue-eyed "gringo" had been hired, the council made it clear, as we have seen previously, that it would back him in the picket line or courtroom in the battle for Mexican-American civil rights and alleviation of poverty among the migrant farm workers he still calls "my people."

Then came the shift—the TCC moved from militant liberalism to "conciliation rather than confrontation." While TCC officials denied that Ed was fired because he refused to exonerate the Rangers, most individuals on the "inside" felt that this was one reason. Still another was the "*viva la raza*" approach to his work which alienated the Establishment and embarrassed the TCC.

The pattern was common. We have already seen how it worked in California's San Joaquin Valley. In many areas, as the predominant religious institutions seek to rechannel their energies to serve the long-neglected, often alienated underdogs of society, those in the power structure want to run the changing program according to their own ways. Dr. Kilpatrick said, "We had the responsibility but no authority . . . but they are not running the program; we are."

Krueger said a basic disagreement with the council resulted from his conviction that "the poor themselves should develop leadership and be helped to a point where they can direct their own lives and determine their own destinies."

Ed's purpose in the valley was not to organize labor unions as he had been accused of doing. Said Ed, "I have not in the past nor am I at present engaged in getting people to join unions. Union activity is not our role."

But early in his valley ministry Ed realized that a notable tendency on the part of those serving the poor was to manipulate them for selfish ends. "One of the dangers of *colonia* organizations is that a lot of people want to use these organizations. One of our rules is to protect the self-identity of the groups to protect them from politicians and from well-meaning people, keeping them from using the *colonias* for their own purposes. Yes, even to protect them from any union official who would use the *colonias* to enhance the labor movement in the valley. What we are interested in is that a democratic community spirit be developed in these *colonias*."

The economic and political power is white and Protestant in the valley. There are names in politics that are Spanish, but the wealthy Latins tend to line up with the Anglos. The Establishment's response to the community organizations was one-sided and harsh. The conservative press, which principally served the traditional Democratic party, delighted in jabbing at Ed, his coworkers, the Texas Council and anyone else trying to change the *status quo*.

Attempts to politically educate the poor were not welcomed. In the Texas general election (November 5, 1968), it was recognized that the state had a long, complex constitution—there were fourteen proposed constitutional amendments. Obviously, these are so complicated in themselves that even the intellectual would have difficulty in understanding the phraseology. Therefore, Ed worked diligently to explain the amendments and to point out how the Mexican-Americans would be involved. He saw this kind of service as urgent because the Establishment had not done the job before and was not attempting to do it.

Despite the denials of pressure against Ed's militant but quiet work among the poor, there was no doubt in the unprejudiced mind that the Council of Churches had succumbed to the Establishment.

Ed knew that his work, especially in the *colonias*, would have political consequences. We talked about this on a visit to a "little suburb." "Naturally, as the poor begin looking at their problems, they begin to understand something about the school board, they begin to notice who their county commissioner is, they see their muddy roads, they call on the commissioner to fix them. Of course they are going to become more alert politically to their whole situation. People who are enjoying illicit power and privilege begin to feel threatened."

Ed makes no apologies for this. He believes reconciliation of conflict is part of the church's mission but that sometimes this has to be preceded by a polarization of differences.

Ed contends that churchmen have long been relating to city hall, county courthouse and other manifestations of the Establishment, "usually to the very serious neglect of the people in poverty." Churchmen so relating, Krueger says, "tend to echo the feelings and thinking of the Establishment."

Ed did not see much success for the TCC's effort to help the poor. "The history of the past sixty years seems to indicate that the churches, as they work with the Establishment, tend to reflect the views of the Establishment, and little or no progress has been obtained for the poor."

Following Ed's dismissal from his job, the Mexican-Americans and some Anglos rose to his defense. In San Antonio, Frank Gonzalez, president of the League of United Latin American Citizens Council No. 2 (LULAC), a conservative group, speaking for the city's entire council, criticized the TCC for dropping its suit against the Rangers. He said that this "constitutes a compromise of principles, and it further has traces of a wholesale surrender to those forces of oppression that have kept the

Mexican-American in lower Rio Grande Valley in conditions of servitude."

Mexican-American groups conducted mass rallies and demonstrations on Ed's behalf although he discouraged confrontation. Some of the picket signs read "The church is for justice. Where is the justice for Mr. Krueger?" and "Is the Texas Council of Churches unChristian?" These were carried in front of the United Methodist Church in Pharr, where the Reverend William Triggs is pastor. Ed described him as a minister who "had conducted an inquisition regarding VISTA." The poor farm workers staged a peaceful vigil in front of the church. But to read the biased news accounts, one would have thought the whole United States Army was on hand.

Bob Boyd, managing editor of the Edinburg *Daily Review,* described events at a Sunday afternoon meeting in Edinburg in an inadvertently amusing manner.

He wrote, "There were at least two direct confrontations between demonstrators and what they call the 'Establishment.' In each case escalation and possible violence was averted by a hair's breath (sic) and a few cool heads on both sides."

The first confrontation occurred when the city attorney, Ralph Vidaurri, arrived with one uniformed officer in front of the United Methodist Church. "They were reinforced by several officers sitting in patrol cars parked out of sight." Vidaurri told those assembled outdoors that they were violating the law. The attorney was "virtually surrounded by several youthful militants, who were apparently unaware of the nearby reinforcements, but cooler heads prevailed . . ."

The second confrontation occurred after the TCC meeting when the police had left. "Two elderly Edinburg gentlemen who apparently attended the TCC meeting got into a fierce street corner type argument with about fifteen demonstrators—mostly young men from 18–25 years of age . . . Insisting that the demonstrators had violated the sanctity of the Sabbath, he [one of the elderly gentlemen] abruptly waved them away and demanded that they 'go back where they came from, and try doing what they should be doing.'"

Harsh words followed, and "several militants fingered his clothing and judging from their mood, came very close to getting more physical with him after the man derided the contribution of the Mexican-Americans in Vietnam."

This is on-the-spot reporting in the valley.

Demonstrations in Ed's behalf broke out all over the valley. The Hidalgo County Political Organization of Spanish Speaking Organizations (PASO) saluted Ed. Abel Ochoa of Edcouch, president of PASO, said, "Krueger's dismissal was a partisan power play. Ed is loved by the unseen poor, the people who never go to a football game, a basketball game or to Padre Island." Ochoa pointed out that the firing would not erase the "problems, discontent and restlessness." He predicted the continuation of demonstrations until changes take place in the valley to improve the lives of the Mexican-Americans.

During a Sunday service in February 1969, a group of Mexican-Americans, members of PASO and the Mexican-American Youth Organization (MAYO), demonstrated outside the United Methodist Church in Pharr. This happens to be the "home church" of Ed Krueger. The aforementioned Reverend Triggs is the pastor. Ed's wife Tina was at the service but left prior to Communion. "I felt I could not participate in Holy Communion because that means forgiveness and I have not forgiven them yet," she said.

The demonstrators arrived while the church was in session and were quiet until the congregation had left the sanctuary. Once outdoors, the congregation was greeted by cries of "*Viva* Krueger" and "*Viva la raza*." At the demonstration Mrs. Krueger wore the red button with the black thunderbird, the symbol of the California grape workers. She explained that the slogan "La Raza Unida" on the button "literally means the united race—a confederation of fourteen Mexican-American groups from coast to coast."

It was not unusual in some of the demonstrations to see signs that read "Don't Buy Grapes," referring, of course, to the California grape boycott.

A special committee headed by Dr. Alfonso Rodriguez, director of the National Council of Churches' Spanish-American ministries, went down to the valley to study the firing of Ed. It was to be an "inquiry of concern."

Said Dr. Rodriguez, "Reverend Krueger was a fellow who had the confidence of the poor Mexican-Americans. Now they have lost their leader. This is one of the few cases where an Anglo is recognized as a leader among the Mexican-Americans." He compared Krueger to Cesar Chavez, leader of the UFWOC in California.

Individuals also came to Krueger's defense. Texas State Senator Joe Bernal of San Antonio wrote to Harold Kilpatrick urging him not to drop the TCC federal court suit against the Texas Rangers. In a letter released to the press, Bernal wrote, "I appeal to your sense of justice. The arrogant methods of the Rangers have been an affront to the citizenship of certain Texans for many years. To compromise with those who still desire the *pistolero* action of the wild west is to encourage other heinous acts . . . As the freedom of one of our citizens is denied, the free-

dom of each of us is threatened." The senator cited Ed as
transcending the "stereotype of many a minister."

Representative Carlos Truan of Corpus Christi also
came to Ed's defense. He asked that the Mexican-American Legal and Defense Education Fund take up the court
suit against the Rangers. "I would like to see the fund
take up the case on behalf of Ed and Tina," Representative Truan said. "For too many years it has been my
opinion Texas Rangers have far too much unlimited
power, and I would like to see the courts rule on the
merits of this case."

What probably meant more to Ed than anything else
was the loyalty and devotion of his wife. She showed her
spunk by sending a telegram to Bishop Pope after Ed's
dismissal. It read, "You publicly stated that Ed had been
dismissed quote for the benefit of the Latin American in
the Valley unquote. I am a Mexican-American, therefore I demand that you retract your statement. For love
of God be truthful. I say it should read quote for the benefit of so-called Christians who repudiated my husband's
type of ministry . . . Do not rely on Triggs' or Reber's
information because you will be disappointed. I prefer to
be penniless than to sell my people down the river. There
has been betrayal. (*signed*) Tina Krueger."

Throughout all of the discouraging days, Tina stuck by
Ed and what he stood for. Even though facing the future
without a job, she, like Ed, maintained her composure.
As a matter of fact, Tina and I enjoyed talking about a
photograph taken out of some newspaper photo morgue
showing Ed at a much earlier age and laughing. As Tina
said, pointing to the February 7, 1969, issue of the Catholic
Messenger, "Look at him. How can he be smiling next to
that headline?" She was speaking about the heading of an

article which read, "Fired minister to stay with poor in the Valley."

Interestingly enough, as the valley issue crystallized, Anglos throughout Texas began to realize how little attention they had been giving to the work of Ed Krueger. As happens so many times, things had been taken for granted.

Probably one of the most thoughtful letters (February 12, 1969) was addressed to Harold Kilpatrick by the Reverend James Angus McLeod of Christ Presbyterian Church in Houston. He wrote, "I grew up in the Valley, and still return to the Valley frequently. My father, though now deceased, when living was a member of the power structure of the Valley. He was a lawyer, yet never made more than four or five thousand a year, with seven children and his mother to support. The reason was that a bulk of his practice was work he did for the *Chicanos* for whom there was no legal assistance provided. In as non-paternalistic a way as could be expected in the early 1950's, he represented many a poor Mexican-American against the Anglo power structure of which, as I have said, he was a part. In the fifties he served as mayor of McAllen. I can remember a few times when he was paid for legal fees in kind by the poor, who wanted to give something, so my father received tacos and frijoles. While it is true that he had no grasp of the poverty rampant in the *barrios* that Ed Krueger is so well aware of, he knew first hand the problems of the *Chicanos*, more so than any other Anglo in the Valley.

"In my estimation he represented the best of the power structure. He, and men still living who run the Valley, have no conception of the extent of the poverty problem among the *Los Chicanos* in the Valley. These are men who make up the Anglo churches in the Valley. Do not kid yourself into thinking that meaningful involvement in the lives of the *Mexicanos* will be forthcoming if a new direction is followed. Ed Krueger is the most relevant servant of Christ ever to minister to Mexican-Americans in the Valley. If what Mr. Krueger says is true, he will continue to minister in the Valley, at some sacrifice to himself, his wife and children. If this proves the case, the Texas Council of Churches has succeeded in nothing more than disconnecting itself from relevance! Congratulations!"

However, the ministers' groups in the valley were strangely silent. Individuals sympathized with Ed, but there was no crescendo of support from the local clergymen.

From Fort Worth, Texas, R. L. Price wrote, "My commendation to you and your wife for a hard fought campaign against discrimination and poverty in the Valley. I regret the action taken by the TCC; yet, you have fought the good battle and are the winner for the exposé of many misdeeds which would never have been revealed except through your gallant efforts."

The Reverend Triggs was not too happy to see envelopes dropped into his Sunday morning offering plates specifically labeled "To carry on true Christianity as taught by Reverend Ed Krueger" and "For Ed Krueger's fund with love. (*signed*) A poor."

The Reverend E. H. Gumper, associate pastor of First Protestant United Church of Christ in New Braunfels, Texas, sympathized by pointing out that at one time he had had to go through an experience similar to Ed's, "standing alone facing a bureaucracy that calls all the shots." He then expressed his opinion about officialdom: "I for one am very cautious to accept the standard formula of officialdom, in whatever instance of 'failure' to do this or that, 'insubordination' and the other stock-in-trade phrases in instances such as yours."

Mrs. Alvina Hayman of San Benito, Texas, wrote, "More power to you in your struggle in behalf of the under-privileged. Would that there were more ministers like you who refuse to sell their convictions for thirty pieces of silver. Keep up the good work as the need in the Valley is great."

Not all letters were encouraging. One unsigned letter to Ed read, "Keep your ass out of union troubles. You are a minister and as such have no right to foment strife, and upheaval and revolt. You are not qualified to understand or participate in business matters. You are not even emotionally qualified, for you are by nature a do-gooder, a faint heart. It takes guts to be a businessman and businessmen have enough troubles without the likes of you ministers. These businessmen support the church, so don't you think it is evil to use their money against them?"

"Ministers like you are destroying the church. Stay in the pulpit and preach about God and Jesus and quit trying to be a labor organizer. (signed) Texan."

I quote these representative letters because they show that most people in the valley and throughout Texas were wise enough to see through all the pronouncements being sent out from the TCC's Austin office. They realized that Ed was fired because of the pressure from the Establishment in the valley.

Furthermore, all of Texas was suddenly awakened to the problems of the valley, whether favorably or unfavorably. So when the new Texas Conference of Churches, an ecumenical enterprise that involved Protestants, Roman Catholics and Orthodox, became a reality on February 24 and 25, 1969, demonstrations took place in Austin at the last meeting of the TCC and the new conference.

Demonstrators carried signs reading "TCC is against Chicanos"; "Texas Council of Churches forgets its Christian mission to the poor"; "the whole world is judging Dr. Kilpatrick"; "If we can't learn power, we'll use human power"; "Pope, Reber, Kilpatrick, traitors of Mexican-American causes—the poor will never forget"; "Reber is a tool of the Establishment"; "We want men like Krueger"; "Texas Council gives in to pressure from valley churches."

One of the last acts of the TCC's final business session was to invite the demonstrators into the sanctuary of First Southern Presbyterian Church and to urge them to make their desires known through their leader, Reynaldo de la Cruz, president of the Colonias del Valle. De la Cruz made an eloquent presentation in which he said in part, "I'm not a very well-educated man. I do not speak English very well. But I would like to tell you in the little English I know what I feel about the Texas Council of Churches. It makes me feel sad when Ed Krueger was fired. Poor people working with Ed Krueger should have been consulted. Poor people should have been consulted about VISTA. The suit against the Texas Rangers should not have been dropped. Some of our people have been harassed—followed to our meetings at night. Why? Why should someone be following our steps? Poor people are not guinea pigs—to be worked with. Only arm we had with the Texas Rangers was the Texas Council of Churches and now the Texas Council of Churches has dropped it. We were told that Ed Krueger was to work boldly with the power structure. We have done this. We marched to the state capital, and the Texas governor was not even there to receive us. He thought it was more important to hunt doves. If the Texas Council of Churches wants to help us, they must help us on our terms without any strings attached. We don't want anyone telling us what to do. We don't want the Texas Council of Churches to hire Ed Krueger back. He would be working with a load on his back—somebody always watching over him."

Despite the gracious reception of the demonstrators, some delegates expressed a fear that the Mexican-American problem was being swept under the rug and that the Texas ecumenical movement was in danger of becoming a missionless movement. At the first business session of the Texas Conference of Churches, delegates passed a resolution submitted by the Reverend William K. McElvaney, of the North Texas United Methodist Conference. It read:

"In an effort to regain the confidence of Mexican-Americans and other groups in the Rio Grande Valley, be it resolved that the first order of business of the board of directors of this historic Texas Conference of Churches shall be to work aggressively, creatively, and to risk its very life toward the goal of authentic mission to these our brothers in Christ."

In an interview with a militant Mexican-American from the valley, I was told that only a few totally oppose the whites. He said that the "power structure" can work in the ministry in a constructive way which considers the thinking and feelings of the poor. The dropping of the suit by the TCC against the Rangers left a feeling of betrayal, for they had thought the churches were backing them. One Mexican-American said, "It is the people with power who wanted Krueger out, not we." An Anglo remarked that the Mexican-Americans regarded Ed Krueger as somewhat of a saint because of his great polarization.

Probably the most astute analysis of the whole situation was given by J. Claude Evans, chaplain of Southern Methodist University, "The problem is old church and old world vs. new church and new world. The old liberals might be called "establishment liberals" (and I do not use the words pejoratively; I've been an establishment liberal myself for years); that is, we have worked through and in the context of the ecclesiastical and social structures of a given period. We were devoted to making changes from within, and we have had many successes. The Texas Conference of Churches is a prime illustration of what establishment liberals can accomplish.

"But a new world is breaking in upon us, often to our great confusion, even to our resentment. The poor organize themselves and, in the words of Reynaldo de la Cruz, ask for help 'on their own terms.' And a new church too is breaking out, in postVatican II forms. Worker priests, poverty ministries, underground worship, ghetto community organizations are experiments outside established church structures—experiments which are even now validating themselves as authentic. Surely the Holy Spirit is active here, illumining the truth that God wills to work his way both inside and outside traditional structures."

Some agree with the chaplain and are flexible enough to change with the times. But along the lower Rio Grande Valley, resistance to change manifests itself in ugly ways. Only the patient determination of men like Ed Krueger is going to sway the consciences of their brothers. But change will come either peacefully or through violence; there is no other way.

It may come most severely from the Mexican-American youth. Those who have returned from Vietnam will demand change. The youth are showing a basic impatience. There is among them a potential for violence. Those who have come back from the war are bitter and antagonistic. They risked their lives for democracy and then cannot come back to anything but closed doors, closed opportunities and closed jobs. When I talked to these men in the valley, I could feel their hostility for things as they are.

As Ed said, "Backing away from the problem will do us no good. It will make matters worse. The voice of the young need to be heard a lot more throughout the entire community as well as the nation."

WOODY GUTHRIE wrote in 1940 that "the worst thing that can happen to you is to cut yourself loose from people. And the best thing is to sort of vaccinate yourself right into the big streams and blood of people. To feel like you know the best and worst of folks that you see everywhere and never to feel weak or lost, or even lonesome anywhere. There is just one thing that can cut you off from people, and that's any brand or style of greed. There is just one way to save yourself, and that's to get together and work and fight for everybody."

Perhaps the fact that Ed so wrapped himself up with the poor was his biggest fault. At first he fought for everybody but failed to manipulate the rich to help him correct the evils that plagued the Mexican-Americans. But Ed is a difficult guy to work with. Like many young Americans, he cannot indulge in sham. He vaccinated himself into the very life bloodstream of the poor. He is not an organization man. He is strictly a people-to-people sort of guy.

When I last saw Ed, he told me he was going to stay in the valley, if necessary to move from his modest home in Pharr to a tiny house in one of the *colonias* that had been offered to him by a Mexican-American friend. "We are used to such a home," Tina told me. "We lived in mud huts for three years as missionaries in Honduras. Our people will take care of us. Material goods don't matter."

Ed's salary was picked up for the balance of 1969 (February through December) by the Board for Homeland Ministries of the United Church of Christ. After the year ends, who knows what will happen? One thing is certain. The Rio Grande Valley is not going to be the same. The poor Mexican-American—from Texas to California and all over America and even the hemisphere—is in a state of flux. Time will make of Ed a hero; there will be changes which may be greater than the growers, the power structure, the Establishment and the unions and *colonias* can cope with.

The situation in Texas is fraught with peril and promise. Those thoughtful individuals in the valley ask: Has the church again arrived on the scene with too little too late?

In answer, we may back off from the sweeping wind and retreat into a shadowy past. Or we may step with men like Ed Krueger into an open valley and share the free currents of the new world.